BYLEVELD

Hanlie RETIEF

BYLE-VELD

Dossier of a serial sleuth

Translated from the Afrikaans by Elsa Silke

UMUZI

The material used in this work has largely been taken from interviews with
Brigadier Piet Byleveld, and court and official police records and dockets. Where
this is not the case, the author took reasonable steps to verify the correctness of
the material.

Published in 2011 by Umuzi
an imprint of Random House Struik (Pty) Ltd
Company Reg No 1966/003153/07
80 McKenzie Street, Cape Town 8001, South Africa
PO Box 1144, Cape Town 8000, South Africa
umuzi@randomstruik.co.za
www.randomstruik.co.za

First edition, first printing 2011
Second printing 2011
Third printing 2011
Fourth printing 2012
9 8 7 6 5 4

ISBN 978-1-4152-0143-5 (Print)
ISBN 978-1-4152-0315-6 (ePub)
ISBN 978-1-4152-0316-3 (PDF)

The lyrics on pp. 9 and 35 are used with permission.

Acknowledgement for the use of images is given as follows:
Beeld: pp. 12 (bottom right and left), 17, 23, 51 (bottom right and left), 53, 65
(bottom), 102 (bottom), 151 (top), 189, 205 (top left and right), 209 (bottom left),
229 (bottom) and 253 (bottom); Rapport: pp. 51 (top), 253 (top right).

Cover design by publicide
Cover photograph of Piet Byleveld by Herman Verwey
Author photograph by Ronelle Meyer
Text design by mr design
Set in Janson Text
Printed and bound in South Africa by Paarlmedia, Jan van Riebeeck Avenue, Paarl

Ook in Afrikaans beskikbaar as Byleveld: dossier van 'n baasspeurder

Contents

To Izak, Jan and Zak

My name is Piet Byleveld
And I'm the cop who cares
Deliver us from darkness
Just one more time
I feel like a lover, left in the lurch
By the hidden truth of wicked crime
In the dives of the black night
I will shine
In the darkest hide-outs we will shine
You see I see with my eyes
You see I feel with my heart
The search for pure thoughts is every man's struggle
Every man has a choice
Every murderer his time
I hear suspects breathing in the last gasps of the night
Every man's soul is naked on the scaffold of his conscience
I walk a path scattered with the boulders of crime
I see angels in the squatter camp
And devils in the boardroom
I hear the whispered wisdom and I have to say it loud
This thing will get the better of us if we take it lying down
In the dives of the black night I will shine
In the dark hide-outs fear will disappear
Yes my name shines in *Beeld*
And they say I'm everyman's hero
But you can just call me Piet Byleveld

Translated version of the song "Byleveld" by Radio Kalahari Orkes

Prologue

In the heat of the Gauteng summers I followed the trail of this
weathered old sleuth. We usually met in December. At our first
meeting, in 2006, he seemed guarded, ill at ease, nervous about our
mutual project. Piet Byl knows all about writing dockets, after all,
not books.

We met in deserted offices or at busy airports, anywhere we could
find a spot to work. He delved into file after file from his memory,
and we trawled through docket after docket from his past.

As one season followed another, I watched as Piet grew in stature.
I stood alongside him as a man turned into a legend.

He is regarded as South Africa's most successful detective, with
a ninety-nine per cent success rate during his career that spanned
almost forty years until his retirement in July 2010.

While his breakthrough in the Leigh Matthews murder case gave
him star status among white South Africans, it was Piet's investigations into serial killings that earned him love and respect among
black South Africans. Letters to the media and comments on the
internet voiced a plea similar to those that were emblazoned on ban-
ners held aloft during protest marches in townships: We want Piet!

In a crime-ridden society, Piet became a symbol of honest, effective law enforcement. He was even the inspiration for the character
Captain Pote du Toit in *Erfsondes*, played by Ian Roberts.

The longest-serving member of the notorious Brixton Murder
and Robbery Unit, Piet was also the only remaining member of
the former unit who was still in the police service by the time he
retired. During the apartheid years, his close working relationship
with his black colleagues gave him the nickname "Piet Kaffir".
His transition from the old order to the new South African Police
Service was seamless.

The FBI, Scotland Yard, the Canadian police and Mossad all

Piet Byleveld, December 2010 in England.

approached Piet for assistance with their investigations into serial killings.

Shortly before his retirement, the International Police Association (IPA) honoured Piet with a special award as one of the three best detectives worldwide. Together with the Judicial Award of the Department of Justice – which had been awarded to only seven police officers in the past – it was a fitting reward for his labours.

On a lighter note, Piet's career progress could also be gauged by the car in which he arrived: from a Chev Lumina to a silver Mercedes Benz, his pride and joy; from a Bantam bakkie to a powerful Ranger.

Conversely, I watched his private life as it spiralled down towards the final disintegration of his marriage, and during our interviews I occasionally witnessed the distress he felt about the situation.

Then – along came a new love, a new life. The evidence was clear: his shirts went from stark white to flamboyantly striped; his hair, formerly cut straight across the forehead, accentuating the ever-present frown, was suddenly styled in a side parting that was more flattering to a face that often beamed with affection in the presence of his new blonde love interest.

Those December conversations form the backbone of this book. This is not a biography; rather, the focus is on Piet's years as a detective and the cases he has been involved in. These are Piet's stories, his recollections and comments on events, supplemented by interviews with his colleagues, newspaper reports, dockets and statements.

During his long career, Piet initially specialised in residential and bank robberies, as well as the murders of police members. What put Petrus Erasmus Johannes van Staden Byleveld squarely on the international stage, however, were his investigations into serial killings. Those were his great success stories, the stories that would eventually define his career.

It all began in 1991 with two cold-blooded good-for-nothings in a hotel bar …

SODOM IN THE DRAKENSBERG

Sixteen-year-old David Sehmel is standing at the roadside in Durban, trying to get away from the Excelsior Place of Safety, from which he has just escaped.

A car stops. He gets in.

This would turn out to be the biggest mistake of his life.

The two men in the car drive away from the city with their passenger. The younger man is attractive, well built, and with a refined appearance. The other one is big, bald and macho.

They drive in the direction of Estcourt, towards the Drakensberg.

Later they stop, unload camping gear, and walk deeper into the mountains with the boy. They climb a few grass-covered slopes and eventually pitch camp on the banks of a stream in a deep kloof.

The younger man sodomises the boy, after which the bald one takes his turn. When it is over, they strangle David Sehmel.

The two men are hungry. They slice some meat from the dead boy's buttocks and have a braai, as casually as if it is lamb chops that are on the menu.

Months later, Piet Byleveld asks them what it felt like to eat a person after sodomising him.

"It was just meat," the bald man says without a trace of emotion or remorse.

It was just meat, and they were hungry.

David Sehmel was just a child ... who happened to be in the wrong place at the wrong time.

Piet Byleveld leans back in his chair, facing me.

The jacket hangs loose on his frame. A copper bracelet, shiny with wear, is visible under the shirt cuff. In the sober, dark suit and white shirt (always the white shirt), his neck scrawny in the tight collar, he might have been a leading elder in a church. Or an undertaker.

His upper lip sports a bristly grey moustache, his cheekbones are high and his short hair is cut straight across the forehead. His hands lie folded in his lap, relaxed, the ubiquitous cigarette held loosely between the fingers. A wisp of smoke drifts lazily upward.

From under heavy eyelids he's assessing me, this civilian who is going to write his book. His eyes are dark, dispassionate behind smoky lenses.

It's December 2006.

We are sitting in the belly of a building somewhere in Randburg, in an empty office borrowed for the day from a friend. Everyone is celebrating Christmas; here it's just him and me and a few pigeons strutting on a windowsill.

Piet casts his mind back to a Saturday afternoon in 1991.

Like every other Saturday, smoke hung over the building of the Brixton Murder and Robbery Unit in Johannesburg, in the shadow of the Brixton Tower. The men were having a braai. Lamb chops and Lion lagers and a 9-mill on the hip.

Earlier, they had searched the cells for firearms and sharp objects, to prevent any attempts at escape. All the bedding had been carried out and the cells hosed down. It was Saturday: cleaning day, inspection day.

Piet was on standby. The telephone rang. On the line was a waiter at the Boksburg Hotel, who said that two men were sitting there discussing a murder in Knysna. It didn't sound as if it was just the booze talking; something didn't feel right.

"My interest was immediately aroused. I must say, I seldom ignore information from the public, but that afternoon I just had a feeling, so I rushed over there."

On his way, Piet recalled the American student Edward Perlmutter (24), who had disappeared on the Outeniqua Hiking Trail near George in October 1991. His mysterious disappearance had made headlines worldwide, and Piet had followed the media reports with interest. Now he had a nagging suspicion: what if these two men turned out to be the killers of the unfortunate student?

Three words on a murder docket always frustrated the hell out of this wiry detective: "Untraceable – docket closed".

When Piet arrived, Juan Havenga (17) and Tony Wessels (30) were still sitting in the bar, talking, drinking hard. Piet arrested them on the spot. Havenga began to tremble. Piet searched their car and found three knives, an axe and a revolver. Bingo!

At the Boksburg police station, Wessels became increasingly upset. When Piet informed him he was from Brixton Murder and Robbery, his meaning was clear: don't even think of making trouble.

Piet said later, "The bastard threatened me. 'If you touch me, I'll kill you,' he said. Wessels was a big, slovenly man.

"I answered: 'You haven't got what it takes.'

"From Havenga's manner, I suspected he was gay. So I took lover-boy aside."

Piet put Havenga in a chair and perched on the table, facing him menacingly. He took out his Parabellum and slowly placed it diagonally behind him on the table. Far enough, but close enough.

"I said: 'I have information that you've been discussing a certain murder in Knysna. We know the story. I'm from Brixton, so don't waste my time.'

"Just that.

"Next thing, he burst into tears and spilled the beans."

They had stood waiting in a footpath for the American student, who was singing as he approached. They overpowered him, tied his hands and cut his throat, sitting on his twitching body.

The plan had been to rob him, but it just kind of happened that

Juan Havenga at the police cells in Knysna.

FAR LEFT: *Edward Perlmutter.*

LEFT: *David Sehmel.*

they killed him. They didn't rape him. (Both of them swore to this, but during the trial the possibility was not excluded.)

Piet returned to Wessels and told him Havenga had confessed to the murder. Wessels became extremely agitated.

The former railway policeman from Johannesburg was wearing PT shorts and sneakers. He was macho, bald, with a strong body odour.

"It's always the same. As soon as they start to panic, they stink."

The younger one, Havenga, was from Durban. The two had met at a gay bar, became lovers, and cooked up a money-making scheme with added sexual benefits. They travelled all over the country in their filthy car, in which they slept when they didn't have enough money to book into a hotel. They focused on homosexuals: soft targets, easy to intimidate. There had probably been other victims, but no one ever came forward to give evidence.

Somebody, however, did survive an attack by these two: Clive Newman, from Port Elizabeth, who had been left for dead on the beach at Blue Water Bay by Havenga and Wessels on 12 November 1991. His throat was "slit almost from ear to ear", it was later testified in court. He recovered, miraculously, but – in a strange twist of fate – this Anglican priest was later murdered in Grahamstown in 2009.

On their way to Brixton in the back of Piet's car, handcuffed and in leg irons, Tony Wessels broke down and began to cry.

"He cried like a baby, this big man, suddenly a coward, full of apologies for his earlier threatening behaviour. I told him: 'I have no respect for you. A while ago you were threatening me, and look at you now: bawling like a baby!'"

The rest of the journey took place in complete silence. When Wessels tried to bum a cigarette, Piet roared: "No one smokes in my car. You'll burn my seats!"

Their car was also taken to Brixton, where the forensic team went over it with a fine-tooth comb, looking for possible DNA evidence.

When they arrived at Brixton, the two men confessed to the murder again and agreed to accompany the police to the murder scene.

"This wasn't the first time, was it?" Piet prodded. "There must be other bodies ..."

The can was open and the worms came tumbling out.

Wessels spoke about a teenage boy they had kidnapped in Durban the previous September and killed in the Drakensberg. In November there had been a retired defence force major in Pretoria. They had left him in a bath, covered in blood. They agreed to point out the murder scenes.

What followed was a macabre road trip during which the policemen and the gay couple retraced the pair's murderous trail across the country.

The first stop was Knysna. Wessels and Havenga were in separate cars, each with his own police escort. They had to point out the scenes independently, so that it couldn't later be said that one had influenced the other.

"Somewhere between George and Knysna we went through a gate and deep into the forest. We were on the Outeniqua Hiking Trail. It took them all day to find the place. It was hot – a clammy heat that clung to one's skin."

During the long walk, Piet's leg gave him hell. During a burglary investigation in Bryanston the previous year, he had been wounded in the ankle and the wound refused to heal. His asthma and chain smoking didn't help matters.

Facing me in the empty office, Piet's hand instinctively moves to his ankle. Fourteen years later, the wound is still a problem. Reluctantly, he pulls up his trouser leg for me to take a look.

It's swollen. Purple. Threatening to turn septic. When he notices my concern, Piet mumbles rather curtly that I am not to worry, he'll nurse the leg back to health in due course.

He was shot by the friend of a domestic worker. The domestic worker had been disgruntled about her salary, and she arranged with her boyfriend and his friends to beat her seventy-year-old employer to death with an iron bar in the kitchen.

"I locked up the domestic worker and her three accomplices. The second one shot me, the third one I brought back from Zimbabwe. Don't ever get involved in a wage dispute with your domestic worker," Piet warns, his voice matter-of-fact. "It's the motive behind most residential killings."

We turn our attention back to the Knysna Forest and its clammy heat.

They stumbled, almost by accident, upon the murder scene near Millwood Hut. The first thing Piet saw was Perlmutter's underpants, dangling from a tree.

"You raped him, didn't you?" Piet insisted, but the two swore blind that they had only taken a few rand from him. They had held him at gunpoint and finally strangled him.

The detectives found Perlmutter's clothes under some bushes, the sneakers placed neatly one beside the other. "So precisely next to each other, I'll never forget it," Piet recalls.

Around them it was summer, and the forest was lush with new growth. At a nearby campsite hikers were getting ready to spend the night, blissfully unaware that an hour earlier they had passed only a few metres from a decomposed body.

The killers had left Perlmutter there, exposed to the elements. "Can you believe it? They did the job and walked away."

In the humid forest the body had decomposed swiftly. Identification was impossible. It was a difficult scene to deal with.

Piet and his companions continued along the murder trail, with the Drakensberg as their next destination.

The killers told Piet they had taken a teenage boy from Durban with them the previous September – David Sehmel.

Having reached a spot as close to the murder scene as the police cars were able to go, they continued on foot, uphill, downhill, until they reached the deep kloof near Giant's Castle where Sehmel had been murdered.

"Hell, my leg was painful. It felt like an eternity, a helluva distance. The grass was wet and we kept slipping."

The detectives found clear signs of a campsite. Sehmel's body parts lay scattered around. They were collected and put into a bag.

Piet glared at the two men. "I told them: 'You are going to carry this body out of here.'"

Neither Havenga nor Wessels showed any emotion, Piet says. They spoke about the "braai" as if it had been an everyday occurrence. They said: "We got hungry, we searched for food, then we killed and ate him."

The campsite was so isolated that if the murderers hadn't taken the police there the child's body might never have been found.

During the hike to the campsite and back, a weird trust began to develop between the two killers and Piet. He had instinctively developed a technique that would later typify his handling of serial killers: never judge, treat the murderers with respect, and create common ground that will later lead to a kind of relationship, even a semblance of a friendship. "And then," Piet Byleveld says, "I hit them on the soft spots. If you don't win their trust, you have very little chance of solving the case."

Piet didn't realise it at the time, but that first serial-killing docket would propel his career in a new direction.

Havenga had remained impassive as he stood beside the child's body. Tony Wessels might have been the bigger of the two, but Havenga, with his cold demeanour, was the aggressor. Havenga had sodomised the boy first, and he had been the one to kill him as well.

As they drove back to Estcourt, Havenga grew quiet.

At the police station, they spread the deceased's clothes out to dry. Hair and other forensic samples were taken in an attempt to identify the child.

In the Supreme Court, months later, the defence hauled Piet over the coals for forcing the suspects to carry the body out of the kloof.

The judge said he did not find it strange at all. Did the defence expect Inspector Byleveld to carry the body out himself? He wasn't the one who had killed the child, after all.

From the Drakensberg, the murder trail led to Pretoria.

"The two had met a gay retired air force major in a hotel, spent a nice evening together, had sex with him in his flat, and then strangled him," Piet told me.

Jacob Petrus Joubert (47) was found naked on his back in his bathtub. They drowned him. In court, evidence showed he had been bitten on the nose. The two men left with his money.

"Worst of all was that they seemed proud of their actions," Piet says. Full of bravado, they regarded each other as heroes, as if they had achieved something major in life.

"They were pissed off when they were locked up in separate cells at Brixton. Wessels, especially, insisted on being with his lover. But I couldn't allow it, of course. Besides, Havenga had been the one to confess first, and I was afraid Wessels might blame him and kill him.

"Then Wessels threatened to commit suicide. It's a fact of prison life: people in solitary confinement are inclined to commit suicide because their conscience finally gets a chance to haunt them."

Piet Byleveld wanted them alive, to stand trial in the Cape Town Supreme Court and be convicted, to pay for their deeds.

When the judge brought down his gavel and an enraged Wessels realised that the game was up, he shouted that he was going to kill Piet the day he got out of prison.

Piet looks at me and gives a belly laugh. "He hates me. But he isn't a candidate for rehabilitation. Serial killers never are."

On 2 December 1992 Judge President Gerald Friedman sentenced Tony Wessels to death. The sentence was later amended to lifelong imprisonment. Havenga, being a minor at the time, got

Vrydag, 20 Desember 1991

Twee ontken moord op Yank

Van Ons Korrespondent

KNYSNA. – Die vermeende reeksmoordenaars wat ook moontlik by verskeie homoseksuele moorde in Kaapland betrokke kan wees, het gister hier in die landdroshof skuld ontken op aanklag dat hulle die Amerikaanse stapper mnr. Edward Perlmutter (24) vermoor het.

Mnr. Antonie Wessels (30), 'n voormalige lid van die Spoorwegpolisie, en 'n sestienjarige seun word daarvan verdink dat hulle betrokke kan wees by een van die grootste reeksmoorde nog in Suid-Afrika.

Beeld het verneem dat hulle ook verdink word van verskeie homoseksuele moorde in Kaapland.

Voordat gister se hofsitting met geslote deure begin het, het die Polisie die twee na die omgewing gebring waar mnr. Perlmutter vermoor is. Hulle moes sekere plekke aan die Polisie uitwys.

By hul aankoms by die landdroshof het mnr. Wessels geen emosie getoon nie. Die seun se kop en bolyf was met 'n kombers bedek. Mnr. Wessels het deurentyd probeer om sy gesig van persfotograwe se kameras weg te draai. Albei die beskuldigdes se voete was in boeie.

Mnr. Wessels, 'n fris man sowat van 1,8 m, het klaarblyklik dae laas geskeer. Hy was geklee in 'n bofbaljet, 'n geblomde hemp, 'n olyfgroen weermagbroek en stapstewels.

Die tiener was geklee in stapstewels, 'n kort fietsrybroek en 'n swart T-hemp.

Die staat het aangevoer dat die beskuldiges mnr. Perlmutter op 25 Oktober op die Outeniekwa-voetslaanpad naby Millwood met 'n stomp voorwerp oor die kop geslaan en daarna sy keel afgesny het.

Mej. C. van der Westhuizen, vir die staat, het ook aangevoer dat hulle mnr. Perlmutter van besittings van altesame R1 730 be-

roof het. Dit sluit in 'n kamera, bergklimtoerusting, klere en R250 in kontant.

Landdros L.J. Fourie het die saak tot 24 Februarie aanstaande jaar uitgestel vir 'n beslissing deur die Prokureur-generaal.

Mnr. Wessels word in die gevangenis aangehou terwyl die tiener in die polisieselle aangehou word.

Kapt. Michael Zeelie van die Polisie op Knysna het gesê hulle word afsonderlik aangehou om te keer dat die ondersoek benadeel word.

Die twee beskuldigdes word ook verbind met die moorde op David Sehmel (15) en 'n afgetrede offisier van die Lugmag, maj. Jacob Joubert (47), asook 'n poging om mnr. Clive Newman, 'n sakeman van Port Elizabeth, te vermoor.

Die lyk van David Sehmel is Maandag in 'n vlak graf naby Giant's Castle in Natal gekry. Hy is sedert September vermis.

Mnr. Antonie Wessels (30), naasregs met die bofbaljet, en die sestienjarige seun (onder die kombers) verlaat gister onder polisiebewaking die landdroshof op Knysna waar hulle skuld op aanklag van moord ontken het.

A report in Beeld *on 20 December 1991.*

a lighter sentence – twenty-five years in prison. Piet has had no further contact with them.

This, then, is the story of two cold-blooded good-for-nothings in a filthy car, scouring the countryside for soft targets – with sex as an added benefit, and murder the collateral damage.

There is irony in Piet's voice as he remarks: "They had such a lovely time together, the two of them …"

A few months later, my family and I are climbing Table Mountain from the Kirstenbosch side, up Skeleton Gorge. Halfway up the mountain, we notice a pair of underpants in the bushes beside the path. "Hey, someone lost his boxers," my sons laugh. I take a deep breath. A shiver goes down my spine. I look around, nervously …

FROM SCRAWNY WIMP TO SEASONED COP

On a hill in Auckland Park, Johannesburg, we get out of Piet Byleveld's Chev Lumina. The car is silver. Spotless. Piet washes his car even before he goes driving on a dirt road. And then afterwards, he washes it again.

It's the weekend, and Piet is not wearing his customary dark suit. His shirt hangs over his trousers, Madiba style. On his feet, leather slip-on sandals – typical cop chic – expose pale toes.

In front of us lies the skeleton of a group of old buildings.

"This used to be the police barracks," Piet says. This is where he first stepped out in police boots at the end of December 1970, after completing his training.

He stands with his back against the car, drawing thoughtfully on a Benson & Hedges, smiling roguishly. "I was a wimpy farm boy from the Waterberg – painfully shy and reserved. At high school I resolved to dedicate my life to God, much to my parents' delight. But then Piet did an about-turn … bloody hell!"

After matriculating from Nylstroom High School in 1968, Piet reported for his national service in the defence force as a member of the Engineering Corps, stationed at Bethlehem and Kroonstad.

Away from the cocoon of the Waterberg and his sheltered life on the farm, Piet was suddenly required to stand on his own two feet. He didn't have a car so on weekends he would hitch a ride to the farm and back.

Surrounded by total strangers in the army, Piet surprised even himself when he realised: "Hell, Piet, you're not such a loner as you've always thought."

In due course he was promoted to drill sergeant. The rules and discipline of the army suited him to a T. As soon as he had completed his service, he returned to the farm to tell his parents that his

At the Police College. Piet, far left in the fifth row, his brother Johann next to him.

On the farm.

Piet during border service in Zimbabwe and the Caprivi.

plans had changed. At the coal stove in the kitchen, where the family always gathered, his father, Martiens, and his mother, Marthie, heard that their bright, devout son wanted to be a policeman.

"My dad, in particular, was bitterly disappointed. He had high hopes that I would be going to university."

Piet chose a career in the police instead of the army because he wanted to work with people. "As a policeman, you deal with the public on a daily basis. They depend on you; you provide them with a service. I dig that big time."

Service. Almost four decades later, staring at the ruins of the old police barracks, I can still hear something of that calling in his voice.

"Selection was tough in those days," Piet says. The standard was high. A number of high-ranking officers visited his parents on the farm to take a first-hand look at the way Piet had been raised. His background was investigated.

"It was an honour to be selected to serve in the police force. It was nothing like today, when people are accepted at random."

On 24 January 1970, Petrus Erasmus Johannes van Staden Byleveld joined the South African Police Force. Force number 056121K.

As a student constable at the Rankin's Pass police station near Warmbaths, now Bela Bela, he was commended by the area commissioner for exceptional effort in a murder investigation. In July 1970, he left for Pretoria to undergo training at the Police College, where he was nominated best student in Troop 41, and runner-up student of the year.

Leaning with his back against the car while he is telling me this, Piet flinches anew. "Runner-up … my arse!"

Having completed his training, Piet was immediately assigned to do investigative work. Not once in his career was he required to stand behind a counter or do patrol duty. At the Hillbrow police station, he investigated motor vehicle accidents, assaults and incidents of damage to property.

After only two years in uniform, he became a trainee detective.

Four years later, Piet was a qualified detective. Initially he focused on robberies – specifically those involving stabbings. At last he was in a place where he could show some initiative.

Piet was exactly where he was supposed to be. At about this time, there were regular armed attacks on passengers at Johannesburg Railway Station. One day, Piet was watching as a young lady got off a train. "The next moment a man armed with a knife appeared at her side. He grabbed her handbag and made off. I gave chase. I tried to arrest him, but in the end I was forced to shoot. It was the first time I had ever killed a man."

Piet was twenty-four.

"How did I feel? I felt I had done my duty. It's not pleasant, you don't boast about it, but I did what was expected of me. There was no further crime in that area."

He hesitates before continuing. "As a child," he says quietly, "I would never have imagined, not in my wildest dreams, that I would ever shoot someone. Dead." It had been a terrible ordeal for him when, as a young boy, he'd had to shoot his horse after it had broken its leg.

"It's a barrier one needs to break through," Piet says. "When you lie in bed that night, you wonder: could I have saved that life? It stays with you for a long time. Until the next incident.

"You never get used to killing a human being, you just learn to deal with it. And I have found myself in several such situations. Several."

Piet lights a new cigarette and gazes at the Auckland Park cityscape. He smokes the entire cigarette in brooding silence.

Piet's forefathers distinguished themselves on the battlefield. In the Anglo-Boer War his great-grandfather, Marthinus Byleveld, had been a diehard under General Koos de La Rey. Piet's father, Martiens, brought back a few medals from El Alamein and Tobruk after the Second World War. The first Byleveld farm was at

Pentonvilla near Ellisras, a cattle farm Martiens, as a returning soldier, received as a gift from the Smuts government. Piet was in standard three when they moved to the farm Weltevrede, near Alma, where his father had established crop farming.

Everyone in the Waterberg knew him. He was chairman of the Agricultural Union, a member of the church council and a founder member of the ultra-conservative Herstigte Nasionale Party (HNP), together with his friends Jaap Marais and Albert Hertzog.

Mom Marthie was also a go-getter – chairperson of the Women's Agricultural Union in her day.

The businessman and rugby-boss-to-be, Louis Luyt, was a personal friend of the family, and he often spent a night on the farm. Another good friend of Piet's father was the former Minister of Agriculture, Hendrik Schoeman. Conversation was limited to agricultural matters, however, as the two men didn't see eye to eye on politics.

Brought up by a strict, religious father, the young Bylevelds were no strangers to hard work. Instead of going away during school holidays, they worked on the farm. Piet was past the age of twenty-one before he had his first glimpse of the ocean.

"My childhood prepared me for hard work, for working without letting up. Tractors. Ploughing. Planting," Piet explains.

It was a hard life. In winter, when Piet and his two brothers worked in the fields, it was sometimes so cold that they peed on their feet for a little heat.

One Saturday afternoon he and his brother Willie, who was two years his senior, grew tired of working. Their father insisted that they finish planting a maize field before dark. No way, they decided, enough is enough. Back at the house, they were given the thrashing of their lives and chased back to the field to complete the task.

Occasionally, the farm workers failed to turn up for the milking on a Sunday morning and the three boys had to pitch in. One morning the three brothers dared to declare a strike, but Martiens walloped them all the way from the house to the milking shed.

"So, yes, I'm used to hard times. My childhood probably prepared me for the difficult road ahead, dealing with criminals."

The discipline he learned at home was a defining influence in Piet's life. "I learned to have a healthy respect for everyone – myself, my fellow man and my superiors. Even murderers. I respect their humanity, though, not their actions. It's not my place to judge, the Great Judge will decide," he tells me. With a nicotine-stained finger, Piet points skyward.

And then something happened that would change their tranquil farm life completely. Johann, Piet's brother, remembers: "A garden worker took my sister, Elize, into the shed and hanged her with a piece of galvanised wire. She was just three years old. If my mom hadn't by chance walked in on them, my sister would have died. My father was beside himself with anger, and would have chopped off the attacker's head with an axe if my mother hadn't talked sense into him. The attacker was later sentenced to fifteen years' imprisonment. The incident was quite a sensitive issue in our family."

Willie says it's something they never talked about. Elize can't remember the incident and Piet says he erased it completely from his memory. "I don't even have a faint recollection. It didn't have a big influence on our lives."

But did it? Was this not an unconscious trigger that made Piet become a detective, hunting serial killers whose preferred way of killing is by means of strangulation? He shakes his head. "No. It wasn't the reason I joined the detective squad."

After all these years Piet's heart is still on the farm – not as a farmer ("I farm in my garden, and I farm with criminals") – but he loves being in the veld, preferably on horseback. As a child, Piet would often get on his horse and gallop into the veld with Bakkies, his boerboel.

His eldest brother, Willie, is an engineer in Ellisras. "Willie is an introvert. He doesn't really communicate. Like my father's people, he is grumpy and reserved," Piet laughs.

Johann, who is a year younger than Piet, farms at Bela Bela. "Johann's difficult too," Piet tells me, "but at least he and I talk. When I get the chance, I pay him a visit."

Piet and younger sister Elize see each other almost every weekend. She and her family live in Johannesburg.

Of the four children, Piet was the softie. "But I think I've managed to show them a thing or two," he grins. "Today I'm the toughest of the lot!"

His first memory is of being a lonely child, the one who would cling to Ma Marthie's apron strings while the others were playing outside. He would help her knead dough and go along with her to the garden to pick vegetables: potatoes, beetroot, whatever was in season.

His mother was always well groomed, he remembers, neatly dressed, her hair black, her lips red. "Sweet-tempered towards my difficult father. They had a wonderful relationship. I can't remember them ever having an argument."

To crown it all, Pietie wore spectacles from the age of six onwards. "I was a pathetic, scrawny runt compared to my sturdier brothers."

His brothers teased him mercilessly, because he was butter-fingered as well.

He's still like that, he admits, embarrassed. Don't ask him to fix something. "I'm always afraid of making a mistake. I get nervous when someone is watching me, and I drop things, believe me."

This is probably the result of what became a regular occurrence in the shed at Weltevrede. When the boys handed their father the wrong tool, he would throw it back at them. "You didn't dare hand him a number ten spanner if he'd asked for a number eight!"

Suddenly the touchy old gumshoe appears ill at ease. The conversation has become too personal for his liking. "You should talk to my sister if you want to know about the Bylevelds," he mutters.

Lunchtime. We are at Tony's in Randburg, with Piet's younger sister, Elize Louw. It's the weekend and the atmosphere is upbeat.

Elize, an attractive brunette, works in the life-insurance industry.

"Yes, my boet," she says affectionately, her eyes following Piet. He's on a mission to the counter for more Amstels.

"My neat, friendly brother. My nice brother. Really," she smiles. "We're still just as close as we were as children, despite the five-year age gap."

She sketches him in a few words: fanatical about the Blue Bulls, his garden, his dogs, braai and beer. Never the centre of attention at a party but a nifty dancer. Incredibly proper in everything he does. The kind of young man every mother wanted as a son-in-law.

"Ma Marthie's blue-eyed boy. He carries her family name, the whole caboodle. That urge to serve the community he got from her. Every morning our mother used to give breakfast to eight poor children, who walked across our farm to catch the school bus. It was never for show; she was simply always there for others. An incredible lady.

"People who have known Piet since childhood and know his softer side often ask me how he can deal with his incredibly tough life, but they don't understand. For Piet, it's all about the victim and the help he can give the next of kin, even if it's just by saying: 'I caught the murderer for you.'

"His work has toughened him over the years. It's been gradual but he has changed, though in essence he's still the same."

Piet wasn't strong as a boy, she tells me. He was often in bed with asthma. But at high school he began to excel at sport. He also read everything he could lay his hands on and did well at school, especially in maths and accounting.

"Our mother died at the age of fifty-two, after suffering a stroke on the farm. It hit us hard."

Yes, Piet recalls when he joins us again. He was busy with an investigation in Durban when he got the call. She was so young …

The Waterberg is still the heartland of the Byelvelds. Their parents are buried at Nylstroom. Piet and Elize occasionally get in the car and drive there, just to say hallo.

His marriage, yes, well, that's a different story, Piet remarks, as we drive away from the restaurant.

In 1971 Piet met the woman who was to become his wife, when he was working at the Hillbrow police station. One evening when he was on duty, the railway police phoned to say there was a problem: a young nurse, who had travelled by train from Cape Town, had had her luggage stolen.

Piet was sent to handle the complaint and met Esmie Dumont, a petite blonde nurse. A few days later she phoned and asked him on a date. A year later they were married.

"Yes," Piet says laconically, "I married a complaint … "

The marriage was a fiasco, a disappointment right from the start. For years, he says, his marriage was like a charge sheet.

She mislead him by not revealing her previous marital status and age.

The Byelvelds hosted a twenty-first birthday party for Esmie on the farm. All the family members and friends were invited, Elize remembers. "My parents were prominent and respected members of the community. Early on in Piet's relationship with Esmie, my mom started worrying because Esmie would contradict him on quite a number of occasions."

When Elize started working at Sanlam, an insurance company, Piet asked his sister to help him with his insurance. "That's when I discovered that Esmie was actually twenty-eight. In fact, my parents had given her a twenty-eighth birthday party on her so-called twenty-first!"

When Esmie's brother and his family came on a visit, the

Bylevelds were surprised to hear them address Esmie as "Joey".

"Why didn't you run?" I ask.

Piet's hand goes to his mouth. He shakes his head slowly. "In those days, in the police force, one had to apply to get married. There was a formal procedure. The personal details of the bride-to-be had to be filled in on the application. Bloody hell, her name turned out to be Johanna Helena Josina de Beer, born on 23 December 1943. She was seven years older than she had led me to believe."

Of course he no longer wanted to marry her when he discovered the magnitude of her deception, but by then his application had been approved. He wasn't keen to withdraw it because he feared it might damage his reputation.

"I was afraid they would suspend me if they found out about her lies. What kind of policeman allows himself to be taken for a ride like that?" He shakes his head ruefully.

Besides, Piet says, in a conservative family such as his own, it would have been considered shameful to get cold feet at such a late stage. He was simply too embarrassed to do anything about the matter. In the Byleveld family the idea of shotgun weddings and divorces most definitely was not entertained, Elize adds.

The die had been cast for Piet Byleveld, so he gritted his teeth and pushed through with the wedding plans.

At Esmie's insistence, they got married in the magistrates' office in Johannesburg on 2 October 1972, instead of in a church, which would have been what Piet had been raised to expect. None of his family was present. To crown it all, he found out on his wedding day that he was his brand-new bride's third husband.

Elize says she will never forget that day. "It was Friday afternoon 6 October 1972. I was in standard nine and my mom had fetched me, as always, at boarding school for the weekend. We had been at home for about half an hour when Piet and Esmie pitched up out of the blue. My mom went out to meet them, utterly surprised because Piet always called before visiting. My dad was busy in the barn and also went to greet them, but after a minute he abruptly turned around and went back to the barn."

Elize sensed that something was seriously wrong because her mother was upset and her father was livid with anger. "All I could get out of Mom that evening was that Piet and Esmie had got married. My parents were seriously upset, and with good reason."

At every family get-together, Elize says, everybody always wondered whether Piet and Esmie would attend, and if so, with whom Esmie would pick a fight. Or would she, as often happened, develop some kind of an ailment, leading to her and Piet's early departure?

There was no honeymoon either, and for more than thirty years Piet has been trapped in an unhappy, childless marriage. "I was so caught up in her web of lies that I truly didn't know how to extricate myself. We have been living a lie.

"It's by far the biggest mistake of my life," he says huskily.

Was it? I can't help wondering.

If Piet had been happily married, with a wife and children waiting at home, would he have spent so many long, lonely nights at murder scenes? Would he still have got married to his dockets?

When he joined Brixton Murder and Robbery in 1977, it was another nail in the coffin of a shaky marriage. Even police marriages that were more stable than Piet and Esmie's often proved unable to withstand the demands of that formidable unit.

RUNNING WITH THE BIG DOGS

Hear the signals from the Brixton tower
Follow the rhythm of the barking dogs
Hear the sirens of one zero triple one
Hear the shots fired in Westbury
The cents of a beggar, the rands of a pusher
Don't buy the peace we're all looking for

*Translated from "Brixton-dae", by the Brixton
Moord en Roof band*

*Brixton's "bush conferences". From left to right: Willem Steyn, Staal
Burger, Kallie Carlitz and Piet.*

Piet (third from right) and Brigadier Manie van der Linde (far right), with Ross Rossouw between them at Brixton Murder and Robbery.

Piet (second from right) with colleagues.

We drive into the parking lot at the Brixton police station. It's an unimpressive building. Grey. The oppressive history of many years sticks to it like the greyish paint on the walls.

As we drive up, Piet becomes alert, almost excited. "This used to be my life," he says as we walk towards the entrance.

He's on a roll. "This is where we used to keep the big dogs. The main criminals. The really aggressive ones. They showed us no mercy, and we showed them none."

The Brixton Murder and Robbery Unit of the former South African Police was known in popular speech simply as Brixton Murder and Robbery. Famous, infamous, legendary.

"We were fifty-two detectives. Spyker van Wyk, Staal Burger, Manie van der Linde ... come, I'll show you where my office was." His voice is gravelly. The result of years of smoking. And his asthmatic lungs.

"Carel Coetzee, Piepies van der Merwe ..." With every step Piet takes, memories come flooding back.

"This is my old office. Room 105. It used to be the tea room before they fixed it up for me."

A nondescript office door in a dark, narrow passage. Inside, the graphic pictures of bodies at murder scenes, the photographs of wanted criminals and the city maps with red dots indicating crime scenes have long since been removed.

When the day arrived in 2001 that Brixton Murder and Robbery officially closed its doors because of restructuring in the police, Piet was transferred to Alexandra, a township north-east of Johannesburg.

"It just isn't the same," he sighs. "Brixton was renowned all over the world. I'm not exaggerating. Scotland Yard, the FBI, everyone came to this little office to ask for my advice on serial killings."

It was every detective's dream to work at Brixton. The selection process was notoriously stringent, and once you were selected, you underwent a trial period of up to a year.

After Piet had completed his training as a detective, he was stationed at the Hillbrow detective branch between 1974 and 1977. During this time he also did a stint on the border, in Zimbabwe and the Caprivi. Shortly after his marriage, he spent four, five months away from home. "I grabbed the opportunity. I wanted to get away from my wife," he admits.

Border duty put the men through the mill. They had to be self-sufficient and survive for weeks on canned rations and whatever game they managed to shoot.

The rules for border duty were simple: "Shoot the other guy before he shoots you. Survive. The experience made me stronger."

The men of Brixton Murder and Robbery took note of the new, tougher Piet Byleveld.

When he arrived for his selection interview on 1 June 1977, he was a bundle of nerves. "Besides," he grins, "my wife had thought she was doing me a favour by buying me a snow-white suit for the occasion."

Piet didn't even get past the charge office before the ragging began. Warrant Officer Frans Horrocks gave him one look and said, "Boet, we don't dress like dollies here."

When Piet entered the interview room, he offered a hasty apology for having got the dress code wrong. Never again would Piet Byleveld be caught without his dark suit, white shirt and tie. Thirty years later, it had become his trademark, like the grey raincoat worn by Columbo, that absent-minded TV sleuth of the 1970s, who could solve any murder that came his way. As a matter of fact, Piet's colleagues did call him Columbo behind his back.

At twenty-seven, Piet was the rookie in the unit; the rest were hardened veterans, all of them thirty-plussers. He knew Brixton's reputation all too well; knew how many young detectives had been chewed up and spat out there.

It was no place for a new boy in a white suit.

Some of the uniformed men in the charge office weren't even prepared to work with the hardened criminals in the Brixton's cells.

"And all that was asked of them was to do rounds!" Piet grins.

Brixton had an unwritten law: prove your mettle, show us we can depend on you, and you'll be accepted in the team. Don't play car guard when the others are chasing after robbers. "You had to be prepared to risk your life for your partners," Piet says.

After a mere three months Piet was given a permanent appointment.

"Then the hard work began. We had to be available around the clock, show what we were made of. There was no mercy."

Divided into groups under the command of an officer, they worked week-long shifts. Every single crime scene in twenty-two police sections had to be investigated in person. Every available member of the unit had to be at a crime scene; the only acceptable excuse was hospital or court. Increasingly, Piet's work turned into a lifestyle. He came home later and later in the evenings. Weekends became mere extensions of the working week.

"Children? I would have liked to have had them, but somehow the subject just never came up."

In fact, Piet's marriage was in deep trouble.

What Piet found most difficult was Esmie's refusal to visit his family on the farm. As a result he was never able to spend a Christmas with them. "She tried to drive a wedge between my parents and me. By 1978 it had become so bad that my father refused us entry to the farm two weeks before my mother's death."

After years of conflict, Piet decided he could no longer live a lie. He discussed his marital problems with his family. Elize and her family became a haven for him in Johannesburg, somewhere he could escape to when things became too difficult at home.

Piet's first big test at Murder and Robbery came when he received a last-minute order to accompany a few colleagues to Bergville in the former Natal. They were hot on the trail of a gang of robbers.

They drove up to a Zulu kraal at night. As they were getting out of their vehicle, shots rang out. They returned fire, but were obviously outnumbered. Piet's colleague Prins Smit got a bullet in the stomach. Kallie Carlitz stormed into the hut from where the shooting had started, with Piet in hot pursuit. "The moment I entered, I saw one of the robbers pointing his gun at Kallie. Luckily I got him first. I shot him dead."

That night they killed three robbers.

Piet and Kallie rushed Prins to hospital in Ladysmith. He survived, only to be killed later in a shoot-out in Soweto.

That night was Piet's breakthrough. His colleagues realised they could depend on him. Back in Brixton, he was now part of the team, but still not a member of the in-crowd.

He accompanied the Brixton boys to their watering holes, but it was always he who drove his intoxicated colleagues home in the wee hours. "I think most of the guys respected me, they knew I'd be there for them," he says, ever the head prefect.

But Brixton had a way of getting to a guy, and it took its toll on Piet as well. He had never been a drinker, but now he began to crack open Lion lagers at the office pub that the men had fixed up for themselves. This was where they partied after work, or celebrated their success when they'd cracked a big case or when a well-deserved sentence had been handed down. It was on evenings like these that the investigating officer in question had better have an open wallet to hand.

Murder and Robbery, Klippies and Coke.

About Brixton's reputation during the apartheid days as an infamous racist unit, where blacks were unlawfully detained, assaulted and murdered, Piet is careful, tactful, when asked to comment. "Look, Brixton did strike fear into criminals. There were many allegations of misconduct – that we assaulted suspects to get them to confess – but nothing was ever proved. It didn't happen."

Not that they took any nonsense. If there was the slightest

indication that someone was going to shoot, they would shoot first, before the suspect could pull the trigger.

"As in shoot first, ask questions later?" I ask.

He nods. "But the crime levels in Johannesburg have never been as low as during those Brixton years, never before and never since. Unlike today, the criminals knew the cops were in town."

The Brixton Murder and Robbery Unit lived up to its name in other ways too. It was a unit in the full sense of the word. Its members knew where everyone lived, and when someone was out of town for work his wife could feel free to phone the commander if there was a domestic problem – even if it was only getting a child to a doctor's appointment. They were one big family, Piet tells me.

The commander was always in contact with his men and if he noticed that someone had a problem he would take him to a pub so they could talk things over.

Brixton also had its fair share of heartache. "Situations at work," Piet calls them. Things he would rather forget, like when a member accidentally shot a colleague seated in his chair in his office.

Marital problems were part of the package. Some women simply couldn't come to terms with the Murder and Robbery lifestyle. One even jumped in front of her husband's car when he had to go to Cape Town for an investigation. And of course the commander often received tearful calls from wives who wanted to know where their husbands had been the night before. Everyone knew, however, that what happened at work stayed at work.

Stress was Brixton's adrenalin cocktail.

"These were guys just waiting to explode. Remember, Brixton was a unique place, the adrenalin was always pumping. If someone thought a colleague was insulting him, the fat was in the fire."

During a celebration at a hotel after an investigation, a brawl between two detectives ended with both in hospital. That night

Piet got into his car and drove away, disgusted. Street fighting wasn't his style.

One evening, the daughter of a colleague came to call Piet. Come and help us, she pleaded, my dad is threatening to shoot us all.

At their flat, his colleague was sitting in the lounge with his brandy and his firearms. His wife and children were in the bedroom and he was threatening to shoot them.

"His eyes were wild. He didn't register what I was saying. So I started drinking with him. And I don't even like brandy," Piet says.

Between imbibing and talking Piet surreptitiously began to collect the firearms and at last got the wife and children out of the apartment.

"And then we really started drinking. All night. Drinking, I saved a family."

When things became too much for Piet, he would get into his car, head off and sit somewhere quiet. Time out. Preferably in the veld. Listening to soothing music helps.

He would isolate himself for hours. "I cut out. Then I would think only about the case I was investigating; I would concentrate, try to remain focused. When I get like that, people know they should leave me alone. I can get rather overbearing if they don't."

Trauma counselling? Murder and Robbery had their own solution: braaiing in the bush.

"The bush" was anywhere in Johannesburg, actually. About once a month the message came over the two-way radio: we're meeting at a certain time and place. Everyone would come. The secretary would sweet-talk the commander, who would pretend to explode. Later he would turn up himself, with everybody partying till they dropped.

"A chop and a slice of dry bread. No butter – that was way too fancy. No salad. Just bread and meat and brandy and beer.

"Later the black members came too, but I reckon they couldn't keep up with the drinking and went home early."

The braais kept the men together. Cases were solved like

that, advice was asked, plans were made, nonsense was talked.

The office pub at Brixton served the same purpose. Occasionally they would restrict the partying to three times a week but before long it would be the same story – every night, until late. But at seven in the morning everyone was accounted for, hangover or not.

"Brigadier Manie van der Linde always used to roar, 'We're partying now, we're buddies, but don't overplay your hand tomorrow!'"

Manie van der Linde was Piet's mentor. Piet still enthuses about him, calling him "one of the most perfect commanders". When the brig arrived at a crime scene everyone knew the boss was there.

About once a week, as if it were a sporting excursion, the unit went to Soweto after dark, on the hunt for stolen vehicles. There was strong competition to see who had the sharpest eyes, who could find the greatest number of stolen vehicles.

"We didn't take any nonsense from car thieves; we shot them, you know. That's how we kept the crime levels down. Robbers use stolen cars, and when you stop a car thief, you stop him from upgrading later to armed robberies or armed violence."

At Brixton they knew who was responsible for which crimes. The bank robbers were most likely Zulus, such as the notorious Two-Tone Gang, who opened safes with angle grinders. The Xhosas focused mostly on building societies, the Pedis were housebreakers and the Tswanas burgled shops, Piet recalls.

In those days, the Murder and Robbery detectives were a formidable countrywide network, in contact with each other at all times, covering all the crime hot spots. Piet maintains that you can forget about curbing crime – especially organised crime – in South Africa without the use of specialised units such as Murder and Robbery.

"Give the detectives a chance to prove themselves, and to specialise in specific crimes, such as burglary. In that way they expand their information networks and cultivate their fields of interest."

The hours slip past as we sit side by side on the office table, the tape recorder between us, in Piet's former detective's lair, surrounded by walls that would have said a great deal, if only they could speak.

Piet made rapid progress. He began to show up some of the old men. He worked closely with his black colleagues, moving around with them to get information. He and Phineas Gcumisa worked together as a team, every single working day between 1977 and 1993. "I don't sit in an office and delegate. I go along, it doesn't matter where."

His nickname, Piet Kaffir, might have been intended to be tongue-in-cheek, but his modus operandi was one of the main reasons behind Piet's success. It gave him access to townships and information sources that helped him solve one case after another. It also made practical sense – when an informant spoke only Xhosa or Zulu, an interpreter was always close at hand.

One night, in the early 1980s, Piet went to Soweto alone, to meet an informant. Typically, he couldn't wait until the next morning. When Brigadier Manie later found out about it he was furious and threatened to take away Piet's car for a month. Piet could have been shot and killed and no one would have been any the wiser. Those were the days before bleepers or cellphones, when police cars were fitted only with two-way radios.

Looking for Piet Byl? (011) 650-5050, call sign BYOO.

"When you stood off at your home at night you had to make an official announcement on your two-way radio: 'I stand off.' When you went away for the weekend you had to sign a register, leaving information about where you were going and a telephone number where you could be reached."

It suited Piet because he could be contacted if new information about a case became available during a weekend away. In such an event the weekend would be cut short without further ado.

"Total availability, ma'am!"

We laugh. Piet produces a roll of xxx mints from his pocket and ceremoniously offers me one. We suck contentedly.

Piet, I'm told, tends to become rather uptight if his colleagues fail to take the idea of total availability as seriously as he does.

Apparently, he was once waiting for urgent information from an informant and had arranged with the charge office that he would be told the moment the informant phoned, no matter what time of day or night it was.

By three in the morning there was still no word and an exasperated Piet drove to Brixton. "I caught the officer asleep; he'd missed the call. I slapped him right off his chair."

Later, on our way to the building's exit, our hollow footsteps echo through Brixton's long passages.

Of all the tough members of Brixton Murder and Robbery, Piet Byleveld is the only one who has remained in the South African Police Service.

"The last one standing …" he says with pride.

He was able to adapt and make a seamless transition from the former SAP to the SAPS.

Petrus Erasmus Johannes van Staden Byleveld.

"I'm proud of those names. Bloody hell! I don't look like a Byleveld, see, so they gave me all the names of my mother's late father."

Ma Marthie, always so worried about her Pietie's safety, died before her son became a rising star, a legend. She would have been proud of her little kitchen helper. From student constable to constable and later sergeant in Hillbrow, from warrant officer in Brixton to lieutenant after he had completed an officer's course, then captain … It was a long, rocky road between promotions.

His strict father, who had been so disappointed when his son no longer wanted to be a minister, was later very proud of Piet as well.

See, Piet did end up with a congregation after all. They wore orange uniforms and they all belonged to cell groups.

"So," I tease, "is Piet Byl afraid to die?"

The question catches him unawares. He stiffens, replies in a rush: the day he's afraid to die someone had better lock him up in a small room because he'll no longer be able to do his work.

Captain Fearless.

But the next moment, he shows something of the sensitive farm boy who lies forgotten somewhere in Brixton.

"I see the ugliest side of things. I see only death. I deal only with death. The cases I investigate are all negative. Involving dead people. Dead children, dead men, dead women. I see only death. And it motivates the hell out of me to solve those cases. No matter who the victim is, he or she was a human being and that human being is dead."

The work, he adds, has made him colour-blind; in death, the colour of someone's skin makes not the slightest difference.

OF GANGS AND FLOATING LADIES

CORPSES

We're sinking our teeth into steak-and-kidney pies from Tasty's when Piet introduces the subject of dead bodies.

About dead bodies you can't tell him a thing, he says. He literally knows them through and through, in every stage of decomposition.

He knows them even better than the taste of Grandpa and Coke, the cocktail that, during his Brixton years, was pushed across Tasty's counter for him every morning before he drove through the gates of Murder and Robbery for another day's work.

Piet is well acquainted with dead bodies.

He sifts through his memory, then tells me that the worst one definitely belonged to the diamond thief who had been lying under a metre of wet Amanzimtoti sand for a week.

"After they had stolen the diamonds in Johannesburg, the robbers fled to Durban, where they shot one of their comrades and buried the body right on the main beach at Amanzimtoti," he says with incredulity.

A week later the detectives were battling to dig up the body. With every bit of progress they made, the sand would cave in again. Hours later they were forced to call in the help of the fire brigade.

"When we got that body out, it was completely decomposed and it had an awful, clammy stench. I had to throw away my suit and shoes afterwards. And it was a new bloody suit too!"

He recalls a "decomp in Garankuwa" – a policeman who had lain in the veld for two months. When Piet picked up the body, the head fell off.

Piet takes a last bite of his pie as we stand on the grimy pavement while the cars swoop past. It's still early morning. Joburg is waking up.

Quite a few times in his life, he tells me, he too has been a mere breath away from becoming a corpse. Like the afternoon when Red

Kekana grabbed him in the back of the police Toyota and started strangling him with his handcuffs. But that's a story for another time ...

When he finally exhales his last (smoky) breath, Piet says, out of the blue, that he dearly wants to be buried in Nylstroom, where his own roots are, where his parents are buried. Perhaps I'm just imagining the hint of nostalgia in his voice.

"Dead bodies are one thing," he continues, "but autopsies, forensic pathology, are really my kettle of fish." He confesses that he becomes quite excited when trying to figure out the jigsaw puzzle of a murder, piece by piece, body part by body part.

"Strange, I enjoy witnessing an autopsy. You know why? I want to know what the cause of death was. I want to know everything. Suspects mustn't come with tall stories. I want to know about all the scratches, stab wounds, strangulations, everything."

Piet was only twenty-four when he witnessed his first autopsy, standing next to the stainless-steel table with the ominous drainage holes.

"You stand tall, ma'am," he tells me.

Autopsies always start early in the morning, at about seven. Just after breakfast. Of course he eats breakfast, Piet says. "And afterwards I eat again. It doesn't bother me; to me it's just a normal procedure – part of the investigation. I've attended hundreds of them."

He can no longer eat boiled sweets, though. Something in the smell, the taste, reminds him of the sweet odour that pervades the forensic laboratory like a thin, green fog.

He has the greatest respect for South African pathologists. "They're among the best in the world. You need a strong stomach to dissect bodies every day, to determine the cause of death.

"But pathologists are a different breed," he says with a grin. Dr Patricia Klepp, a Johannesburg pathologist by whose side he has stood for many an autopsy, always shows him the smokers' lungs, he tells me. "See here, Piet, this is what your lungs look like."

Few jokes are as funny as those around an autopsy table, Piet says. He and Doctor Klepp share a sense of humour that occasionally brought some relief to those morbid surroundings and the lifeless company.

Piet used to attend autopsies in his suit. He could smoke as well, which helped to disguise the smell. Today it's masks and white coats.

"First the body is washed," Piet reveals, before he starts leading me through the pathologist's entire procedure, step by step. "The breastbone is cut open and the heart and other organs are removed. These are cut into smaller pieces and carefully examined. Everything is weighed to detect abnormalities. Injuries – caused by a blunt instrument, a bullet, knife or other sharp object – are examined particularly carefully. It is a tedious, careful process to determine the exact cause of death.

"When the skull is cut open, it sounds like a tree being felled."

Piet notices my face. "Yes, I've seen it all, every piece of the body, everything that can happen to a human being."

Does it make him fear for his loved ones? What might happen to them?

"It does enter my mind, yes," is all he is prepared to say, but he suddenly looks uncomfortable.

Outside Tasty's, in one of those green garbage cans fixed to a lamppost, my pie has found a final resting place. I have taken only a single bite.

THE SHOTGUN GANG AND THE STANDER GANG

The years between 1977 and 1988 were Piet Byleveld's formative years as a detective.

His first major challenge was to detain the notorious Shotgun Gang. In the latter half of the 1970s, this gang, led by Dougie Scheepers and armed with shotguns, robbed several shops and banks in Johannesburg.

"Dirty robberies, all of them," Piet grunts with disapproval.

Two of the gangsters had grown up in the rich northern suburbs of Johannesburg. Drug addicts, wild and lawless, they did exactly as they pleased. When Scheepers shot one of his own men in the leg by accident, he took him to hospital himself.

Later the gang began to target building societies, and Piet and his colleague Spyker van Wyk were assigned to catch them.

The hunt went on for months, but their actual apprehension was over in a matter of minutes. Still, it was also the first time Piet came directly under fire.

"We were involved in a hectic car chase. As we came abreast of them, Scheepers and his men fired wildly. Bullets whistled past. And there was nowhere to go!"

It was like the movies, Piet remembers. A few kilometres further down the road, Piet's team managed to force the fleeing gang off the road, and they rolled their car. It all ended in dust and hand-cuffs. No mercy in this game …

Scheepers was the first white robber to be sentenced to death in South Africa, even though he hadn't actually killed anyone. His death penalty was later set aside.

"But," Piet reminisces, "it was the Stander Gang who really gave us a run for our money."

André Stander was the moustached policeman son of a former general in the corrective services. Blue blood. Charismatic. A born leader. Meant for higher things.

Instead, he became one of the most audacious bank robbers in the country's history. Everyone was up in arms. The newspaper head-lines shouted their outrage.

In the 2003 film *Stander*, the ex-policeman was portrayed as an apparatchik of the apartheid regime who had become politically disillusioned and decided to give the establishment the finger.

Piet with André van Wyk during the Dougie Scheepers case.

Dougie Scheepers.

André Stander.

Piet thinks that Stander was nothing more than a rotten apple in the basket.

"A highly intelligent one, I must add. As a young policeman, I was shocked and humiliated at the thought that a police officer could sink so low." He is clearly disgusted.

Stander had quickly made his way up the ranks of the police force, and before long had been promoted to branch commander at Kempton Park police station, which was conveniently close to Jan Smuts Airport (now OR Tambo International).

On weekends, Stander left his police vehicle at the airport, flew to Durban, put on a disguise, robbed to his heart's content, flew back, and coolly carried on with his work as a detective.

Sometimes he would even rob a bank in his lunch hour, only to return to the same crime scene later – as the investigating officer.

When he had robbed about thirty banks, Stander was apprehended by Manie van der Linde and detained at Brixton Murder and Robbery, where Piet first made his acquaintance. In prison, Stander met Patrick Lee McCall and Allen Heyl. Plans were laid, and on 11 August 1983, having been taken from the Zonderwater Prison for an appointment with a physiotherapist, Stander and McCall overpowered the physiotherapist and escaped. On 31 October they helped Allen Heyl escape, and the unholy trinity hit the Witwatersrand in an orgy of bank robberies.

The media dubbed them the Stander Gang.

On 30 January 1984, Piet and his team received information that Stander was holed up in a house in Houghton. A drove of detectives descended on the place in the dark, took up their positions opposite the house and remained in hiding until the next afternoon.

When a black Ford Perana drove into the property, one of Piet's colleagues could no longer contain himself and began to shoot. The police stormed into the house and shot and killed McCall. But Stander was nowhere to be seen. Later, Piet found out that Stander

Patrick Lee McCall.

Allen Heyl.

The only couch in the Stander Gang hideaway in Houghton was cut open underneath.

and Heyl had already fled the country at the time of the ambush.

On 13 February 1984, when Piet heard that Stander had been shot dead in Fort Lauderdale in America, he was almost relieved. Case closed.

Of course, Piet and his colleagues had to inform Stander's parents of his death before the news hit the papers.

"The old general and his wife didn't receive us well at all. I had the feeling they somehow blamed us for their son's death."

To make matters worse, Piet and his team had to search the house for evidence – including André's ultra-neat bedroom, which was still redolent of the hopes and dreams of a young man, remembers Piet. Hopes of a good life, dreams of a straight and narrow road ahead.

Next they went to Stander's house on the East Rand, where his girlfriend, Becky, lived. She received them with an abrupt and annoyed demeanour, her hands on her hips. The detectives found nothing – until one of them opened up the ceiling and a black garbage bag fell out, filled with cash that Stander had hidden there earlier.

And Becky?

"She was a spontaneous girl, a handful, no, two handfuls," Piet teases as he lights another cigarette.

Residential murders
In the late 1980s, Piet started to specialise in residential murders.

It was a matter of principle. Piet still gets uptight every time he is asked about robberies that have been committed at residential premises.

"I can't stand it when people's privacy is invaded. You should be safe in your own home, able to relax. Then these criminals come, and they pounce when you're at your most vulnerable …

"I had a passion to solve residential murders in those days; it was my first speciality."

Piet was able to solve more than eighty per cent of the residential burglaries he investigated. The inner circle of the police took notice of the young detective and it was during this time that he was promoted from sergeant to warrant officer.

Piet and his old comrade, Sergeant Phineas Gcumisa, were even sent to Natal to investigate residential murders there. "We investigated many residential murders. Many. Many. Many."

Piet always saw to it that he got to the murder scene as quickly as possible. The quicker, the fresher the clues, and the better his chances of catching the killers, he explains. The guys on duty at the station always trusted Piet to come, even in the dead of night.

Every residential murder can be solved, Piet believes, because there is always a motive. In most cases the killer has a connection with the victim – a disgruntled domestic worker or a gardener who feels hard done by about money, who was paid too little, who got his bonus too late. Someone like that holds a grudge and doesn't hesitate to kill.

Piet and Phineas always worked the crime scene together. They conducted interviews at the scene with relatives and any potential witnesses. The smallest detail was followed up: fingerprints, blood, footprints, saliva. DNA evidence only became available some years later.

"In one murder I investigated, the victim was an elderly woman in Bryanston. She had been in the kitchen, eating, when she was struck on the head with an iron bar. I found her broken dentures on the floor, and her glasses – smashed underfoot."

At the scene, Piet became suspicious when the domestic worker, a Zimbabwean, seemed too calm and collected for someone who had just discovered her employer lying on the floor, brutally murdered. He found out that she and her employer had not got along. There had been a dispute about the woman's wages, and she had hired people to kill the old lady. The perpetrators were given a life sentence and the domestic worker was sentenced to a lengthy imprisonment. Proper detective work at the scene of the crime will allow one to solve a case, Piet emphasises.

It was just such meticulous detective work that allowed them to solve another residential murder that took place in Ridgeway, Johannesburg.

In contrast to the previous case, this aged couple had treated their domestic worker well. "They had even bought her a house in Harrismith," Piet reveals. "She got her boyfriend to commit the murders."

Piet found the old people on the sofa, with the TV still on. They had been beaten to death with a hammer. In this case, the domestic worker was crying and screaming so hysterically, Piet realised she was overreacting. He also noticed that the stairs and walls had been wiped clean. He had the surfaces tested and the forensic team found traces of blood. Piet subsequently took the team to the domestic worker's room and there was clear evidence of blood in the basin. Piet also found the bucket and rag with which the woman had mopped up the old couple's blood.

On her way to the police station, the domestic worker admitted that she had asked her boyfriend and two friends to kill her employers. There had been a wage dispute. All four of the accused were sentenced to death.

One particular residential murder that still haunts Piet today involved a seven-year-old girl in Wendywood. His expression is grim as he tells the story.

"It was in 1979. When the little girl came home from school, the gardener was waiting for her inside the house. We found her body in her parents' bedroom. He had slit her throat, and her blood had spurted against the walls of the room, the ceiling and all over the bed. It was a grisly scene, one I'll never forget."

They later shot and killed her murderer – a sixteen-year-old youth – during a confrontation in an outside toilet in Alexandra. He had taken only her bicycle.

"Such a brutal murder for a child's bike." Piet shakes his head in disbelief.

That night Piet had lain awake, fretting about a little girl who had bled to death and a boy that he'd had to shoot, wondering whether he should be doing something else with his life. "The next morning I had to get up as always, but I'd come to terms with the fact that I had had little choice. The youth had pulled a knife and attacked me.

"Residential murders upset me, dammit! Remember, I arrive at the scene and see innocent people lying dead. I see the cruel ways in which they have been killed, the grief of the family. I'm the one who has to tell the family: listen, your daughter is dead. Or your mom or dad. So many times I've had to do it. But it's my duty. The next of kin must be the first to know."

Piet has developed his own method for this: he starts by saying there has been an incident and unfortunately the news is not good. The worst has happened …

Then they know.

Details are not really necessary, so Piet avoids them if he can. He presents the bereaved with the bare facts, unless the full story will later be heard in court. Nevertheless, Piet always tries to spare the relatives the worst details. "You must have empathy, even if this game has made you as tough as nails."

The most difficult part of bearing sad news is dealing with people's reactions, Piet says. Every time it's like a kick in the stomach. People usually react with either hysteria or disbelief. Often they will say something like, "It's impossible, I spoke to her on the phone only a while ago." Then it's Piet's task to convince them of the truth of what he has to tell them, with tact and patience.

He always tries to have the family's minister present, but still insists on imparting the news himself. It's the duty of the police, Piet believes, and in the past the police used to be very conscientious about fulfilling this duty. Nowadays people sometimes read about the death of a loved one in the papers. This upsets Piet, because it's not the way it should be done.

Murder, crime, dockets – hundreds of them – are morbidly filed away in Piet's memory. There are few aspects of the seamier side of life that those small dark eyes have not witnessed. Nothing surprises him any more.

Piet suddenly recollects an old man in Lynmeyer, Johannesburg. His wife had been beaten to death and the man's life was hanging by a thread when Piet and his men arrived at the scene, blue lights flashing.

The human faeces in the backyard told Piet that the killers were youngsters – nervous and afraid.

He and Phineas discovered that the old man had lured boys to the house for sex when his wife was away. He would stand at the front gate and call them over.

Piet caught one of the murderers near Swaziland just before he could slip over the border, and the other one in the Transkei.

CAMARADERIE

Sergeant Phineas Gcumisa was more than Piet's assistant. For many years he was also his closest comrade. He was the man who did a lot of Piet's footwork, gathering information from the community, which, Piet tells me, is so important if you're ultimately going to catch a criminal.

Phineas was one of those extraordinary policemen who preferred patrolling on foot, Piet says. He had dozens of lady friends and the amount of information he could get from the community was astounding. Information through adoration, one might say.

Piet would drop him at the scene of a crime in the morning, and he would patrol the area on foot or by bus. He got his driver's licence only late in his life, after Piet had patiently taught him to drive.

When they went to Zululand, Piet would accompany Phineas to the kraal where he was the headman. Piet would park outside his hut and Phineas' impis would guard the car through the night, while Piet slept inside.

"Phineas had three wives and many girlfriends. He was very active," Piet laughs. "But there were a lot of times when we had to work hard and long. Eventually Phineas would say, 'Please, I have to get to my wives'!"

Those were the apartheid years, when black and white could not stay in the same hotels or eat at the same restaurants. The laws of the country made it difficult for this resourceful police partnership to do its work. But both Piet and Phineas steadfastly saw to it that their work, which took them all over the country, was never compromised as a result of such constraints.

While Piet booked into a hotel, Phineas would find a lady friend at whose house he could spend the night. At lunchtime, they used to walk straight past the restaurants and instead go to a butchery where they bought some meat. Later they would stop under a tree and braai.

"That's how we used to work," Piet says.

Sergeant Phineas Gcumisa retired in 1993. He enjoyed his retirement years in his kraal in Zululand with his wives and family and the elders of the tribe. Not to mention his memories of the time when he and Piet Byleveld used to hunt criminals, of course.

"Yes," Piet says quietly, "eventually he died of a stroke. He was my friend."

After Phineas, Inspectors Ronnie Magina and Lucky Ramaboea became Piet's feet – the team with whose help he would catch some of the most notorious criminals in the history of South Africa.

Informants

Without information from the community, Piet says, a detective can forget about doing a proper job.

In the 1980s the police still had an excellent network of informants.

The identity of an informant (a member of the public who supplies information about crime, sometimes at a fee) is never revealed, or he might end up in a ditch with a bullet in his brain. For this reason, a detective never sees an informant in his office; he meets him on neutral ground. Usually an informant's identity is not even known to the detective's colleagues.

It was generally the so-called "occasional" informants who were most useful to Piet. They are the ones who come forward with information about a specific crime in which they have in some way been involved, often as an eyewitness.

"I don't have much faith in a guy who keeps phoning you with information, who keeps turning up on your doorstep," says Piet disapprovingly. "That guy is a criminal; he's just looking for easy money."

Payment for information depends on the case in question. No prior promises are made about payment because the value of a piece of information can only be established after the fact. The police will pay up to R20 000 for information if it leads to an arrest or a guilty verdict. Should an informant later become a witness, the money will be paid over only after the accused has been found guilty.

A narrow escape

In 1988, officials of the newly established Civil Cooperation Bureau (CCB) approached Piet Byleveld and asked him to join them.

The CCB was a covert division of the special forces of the former South African Defence Force. The aim of the CCB was to infiltrate the enemies of the government of the time, gather information and destroy these enemies and their bases.

The CCB recruited their operatives from the ranks of the defence force and the police, but they functioned under the jurisdiction of the defence force. Police members therefore had to resign if they wished to join the organisation.

In 1990, South Africans for the first time became aware of the existence of the CCB when the Afrikaans anti-apartheid weekly, *Vrye Weekblad*, exposed the organisation's covert activities. The president at the time, FW de Klerk, disbanded the CCB in July 1990. In 1995, during the hearings of the Truth and Reconciliation Commission, South Africans heard shocking revelations about the many atrocities that had been committed by the CCB. Not only was the veil lifted off certain unsolved murders, like those of David Webster and Dulcie September, but gruesome tales were told, sometimes by former CCB members themselves, of indescribable cruelty towards activists, of killings, and night-long barbecues while bodies were being cremated.

A large contingent of former members of Brixton Murder and Robbery were involved, men such as Staal Burger, Slang van Zyl, Chappies Maree and Calla Botha. It was to this organisation that Staal Burger tried to recruit Piet Byleveld.

Instinctively, Piet drove to the farm to discuss it with his father – as he had done before taking every other major decision in his life. He suspected that there were other snakes in the grass besides the one known as Slang van Zyl, his former colleague.

When Piet broached the subject with his father, Martiens Byleveld reacted in his usual cantankerous, outspoken way. He foresaw that Piet might end up in situations from which he would not be able to extricate himself. "Stay away from those people," he had advised Piet. "A Byleveld doesn't belong there."

His father went even further and suggested that Piet resign from the police and come back to the farm. A short time later, he got into his car, drove all the way from Nylstroom to Brixton, marched in and purchased Piet's discharge.

For the next two years, Piet and Esmie lived on the farm. Piet was thirty-eight. He tried farming, but it bored him to tears. He thought he was going to lose his mind.

Then his old friend André de Vries, former Attorney General, drove out to the farm to convince Piet to return to his former job. It took about ten seconds, Piet remembers, smiling. In 1990, at the very time the CCB was disbanded, Piet rejoined the men of Brixton Murder and Robbery.

Later Piet's worst suspicions about the CCB were confirmed. It had been a narrow escape.

"I try to walk the straight and narrow, like my dad. My dad was always straight as an arrow. He tolerated no deviation, no corruption," says Piet and looks me in the eye, directly, unflinchingly.

We stop in the parking lot of the Brixton police station. Piet remembers something and laughs. "You're standing on a crime scene now, ma'am. Right here, Piet Byleveld almost met his Maker.

"In the end it was the other fellow who met his Maker," he adds drily.

"One evening in the early 1990s we booked out a suspect. The guy was hardcore. He was being charged with a hundred and one complaints, including murder and armed robbery. We cuffed him properly, but before I could put him in the vehicle, he struck me such a hard blow with the cuffs, just above my eyes, that I later had to have fourteen stitches. While falling, I saw that he was strangling my colleague. I shot him before I hit the ground.

"Eleven shots, over and out."

Cop killings

During the political changes in the country, in the turmoil between 1990 and 1993, several white policemen were murdered in cold blood in Gauteng.

Piet was tasked with investigating this disturbing trend.

"It was ugly; my colleagues were simply being mowed down, one after another, next to the main routes."

The criminals clearly had no respect for the police. Their main purpose may have been crime, but in the process they seemed determined to kill as many white policemen as possible. Piet is still convinced they had an added political motive.

Under Piet's leadership, a special elite unit of ten members was established to nip this tendency in the bud. They worked from the Sandton police station.

"Except for one instance, we shot and killed every attacker who fired at us. They had no mercy for us, they shot to kill, so we were forced to shoot as well. One day in Rosettenville three of them opened fire on us. The buggers. We shot and killed all three."

But Piet himself almost got a bullet in the head. From a police firearm, inside the Sandton police station, to top it all.

It was one of the buggers, he growls, that they had caught and were taking to the Sandton police station for questioning. The gangster was climbing the stairs behind Piet's colleague. The next moment he grabbed the detective's Beretta, shoved him aside and shot at Piet.

Piet reacted instantly and shot him dead, right there on the stairs.

"One of my bullets is still in the wall," Captain Fearless boasts. In the last incident of that kind, five gangsters ambushed two policemen who were on their way back from investigating a residential robbery in Illovo. They shot and killed one policeman with his own RI rifle and wounded the other.

"I hunted them down. And I found every last one of them.

"My unit had a one hundred per cent success rate," he says proudly.

Piet sits drumming with his fingers on the steering wheel of the Chev. We are waiting at a red traffic light on our way to Sandton.

"There's no respect for human life in this country," he mutters as a red-light vendor unsuccessfully tries to interest him in a pair of sunglasses. The next man gets a slight smile – he's selling Blue Bulls flags.

"In the eighties, the police were feared by criminals, but that's no longer the case," Piet continues, indignant. He hates it when innocent people are harmed. "Every fibre in my body shouts out against it. I hate crime – I always will."

This is the cold white anger, the drumbeat to which Piet Byleveld marches.

"Don't fuck with me." His voice is menacingly soft. "If a criminal does someone harm, I'll get him. I'm not arrogant when I say that."

Did the death penalty help? I ask him.

"Of course it helped. Of course it made a difference. How can it be right to kill innocent people, spend a short while in prison, and go straight back to killing when you get out?"

We drive through the tall trees of Morningside. The residents here live a cushy life – manicured gardens, palatial houses, Mercs and BMWs parked behind cast-iron palisades.

"Over there," Piet points with his finger, "three streets further down, I came across one of the most bizarre cases of my career."

WOMAN IN POOL, MAN ON AUTOPSY TABLE

16 April 1996. A body was floating in a pool in Morningside, Sandton. When the police arrived, they indeed found "a dead, floating lady".

It was like a scene out of a CSI programme – a floating woman in a white dressing gown, her long hair fanned around her head in the turquoise water. At the edge of the pool, a dejected bull terrier kept watch, growling when the police approached.

The victim's name was Carol Donaldson. She was well known in Joburg social circles, the owner of an exclusive clothing boutique in The Firs shopping mall in Rosebank.

When Piet arrived, he saw clear evidence of a struggle: blood in

Piet with Phineas Gcumisa.

BELOW: *Carol Donaldson.*

the bathroom, drag marks in the passage, bloodstains on the snow-white carpet. And there the bloody trail ended. "The only deduction I could make was that she had been carried the rest of the way and thrown into the pool."

As always, Piet attended the autopsy. Dr Patricia Klepp had the scalpel in hand that morning. The autopsy went according to procedure – then they got the shock of their lives.

"Bloody hell – this beautiful woman was actually a man!"

"I would never have believed it if I hadn't seen it with my own eyes. The sex-change was done expertly. She was a real lady.

"As professional as always, Dr Klepp put down her scalpel and then, out of respect for the deceased, the two of us hurriedly left the autopsy room to collect our senses."

Later, Piet would find out that Carol Donaldson underwent the first complete sex-change operation ever performed in South Africa, some thirty years before her death.

It emerged that her live-in boyfriend, Paul Smithers, had vanished into thin air, as had her BMW. At twenty-six, he was exactly half her age.

Just before dawn, five days after the murder, Piet was informed by radio that Smithers was hiding in a cottage at the back of a property in Blairgowrie. That same morning Piet had been in Soweto for the past four hours, investigating an armed robbery. He left that crime scene and hurried back to the suburbs of northern Johannesburg.

"When I kicked in the front door, I found him in the bedroom in his underpants, slashing his wrists. I charged in just as he was slashing the second wrist; blood was spurting in every direction."

Piet pinned the guy down, grabbed a few towels with his other hand ("snow-white towels, I'll never forget") and applied pressure to the arteries. As they forced open the man's hands to remove the blade, he screamed: "Let me go, I don't want to go to jail."

The policeman in Piet immediately realised: the man is confessing his guilt! The next thing he thought was: you'd better not bleed to death; I want you to pay for what you did to Carol Donaldson.

Piet and his colleagues rushed Smithers, who was bleeding all over the back seat, to the Garden City Clinic. Piet wondered how the hell he was going to get all that blood out of his upholstery. "What would it look like if I had to drive an advocate around in a bloodstained car? A man is judged by his appearance and his car."

On the way to the clinic, the bleeding Smithers became increasingly aggressive, wrestling with Piet's colleagues, Lucky and Phineas. "Smithers was only in foot irons," Piet explains. "How do you put handcuffs around slashed wrists anyway?"

While he was fighting, Smithers kept begging Piet to get him to a doctor before he bled to death. Piet, always a man with an eye for a deal, agreed, provided that Smithers gave his full co-operation in the matter of Donaldson's stolen BMW and jewellery.

That afternoon, after his wounds had been stitched, a bedraggled Smithers showed Piet where he had abandoned Donaldson's car.

"When we got to the car, the guy began to cry – another sign of guilt." Smithers also directed Piet to the pawn shop where he had sold his lover's jewellery. However, before Piet could go there, the anxious owner had arrived at the police station with the loot. He had read about the case in the papers.

"According to Smithers, Carol Donaldson had been alive when he had thrown her into the pool. A cruel thing – leaving a person to drown because you don't have the guts to strangle her to death."

According to her sister, Carol met Paul Smithers at The Firs shopping mall in 1993. "They lived together and she was in love with him. But things went sour and he moved out of her townhouse."

They had argued about money, it was said, and Smithers had lost his cool, assaulted her, thrown her into the pool and fled in her car with some of her jewellery.

"It was pure greed. He sponged on her. Later he told me he'd been aware of her sex change but – he had the temerity to tell me – sex between them had been really good.

"I later found out Donaldson had also had a special friendship with a policeman, someone well known to me …"

But Piet's lips are sealed.

Donaldson's sister had apparently warned her against Smithers, convinced that he was nothing but a parasite, only pretending to look for work, but never actually doing anything about it. His hold over the woman was simple: if she left him, he would tell the newspapers that she was a man.

"Apparently she had been besotted with him before becoming disillusioned. That early error of judgment cost her her life."

On 13 May 1997, Smithers was sentenced to twenty-four years for murder, fifteen for robbery, and two years for the illegal possession of a firearm and ammunition. Forty-one years in total.

In the silence that follows I can almost hear the sound of the judge's gavel.

Paul Smithers will probably serve only about twenty-four years, Piet reckons. The last time Piet heard anything of him, though, Smithers was still in Modderbee Prison, somewhere between Benoni and Springs.

Residential murders, cop killings … Then, in 1991, Wessels and Havenga came along, and Piet Byleveld had his first encounter with serial killers. He knew at once: this type of crime is complex, fascinating, deadly – he had found his niche.

It would become Piet Byl's great passion, the one that would make him a legend.

STRANGLER WITH A CONSCIENCE

On Van Reenen's Pass they pull off the road. They're hungry. It's time to eat.

The boot is opened, a braai grid is taken out, and camping chairs. They braai, four detectives and a rape suspect they have picked up at Kranskop in KwaZulu-Natal. They are taking him to Joburg for questioning.

Piet Byleveld has a strange feeling. This little man in the green jersey, his instinct tells him, has done more than commit a single rape.

They begin to talk around the fire, about this and that.

The man is modest, Piet sees, and painfully neat. He offers him some grilled meat.

They eat, with the cars swooping past on the N3.

Piet makes his move. Listen, man, he says to the suspect, you're in big trouble; you're not going to get out of this ...

The suspect looks around, then asks for water.

Piet knows: here it comes. He's asking for water, he's going to talk.

He starts talking, and it turns into a torrent of words.

He tells Piet about the woman at Welverdiend near Carletonville, the schoolgirl at Vrede, the girls at the Kranskop taxi rank.

He raped them all. And yes, he strangled them all.

It turns into a confession around a fire, beside the highway.

If you say the name Bongani Mfeka, you will see a softness flicker in those slightly Slavic eyes beneath the hair that is cut so straight across Piet Byl's forehead.

In the world of serial killers, the thin, unassuming Bongani Mfeka was unique. Piet knows of no other serial killer who showed remorse for his actions.

Mfeka begged Piet: "Don't ever let me get out of prison, because I'll kill again. I can't stop myself … Lock me up, that's where I belong."

The seed of evil was sown early, during Mfeka's troubled childhood in the hills of the former Natal, in a hut near the Kranskop.

Mfeka's father couldn't stand him. He was cold and distant towards his scrawny young son. But it was Mfeka's mother who was the head of the household, domineering, and overprotective towards Mfeka. They developed an unnaturally close relationship.

During Mfeka's teenage years, their relationship became increasingly warped. His mother sometimes helped smuggle girls into his room without his father's knowledge. Piet later heard from the mother that Mfeka sometimes had two girls in his bedroom at the same time.

"That is where Mfeka's troubles started – his absent father, his weird, domineering mother, a classic breeding ground for a serial killer," Piet assures me.

In almost all the serial killings Piet has investigated, something had inevitably gone seriously wrong with the killer's sexual identification as a child.

"But that's not enough reason to go out and kill women," he says, repeating the words you hear him say so often.

Here in his friend's garden flat in Randburg, we are surrounded by files stacked high on two tables, together with a laptop, a few Amstels and Coke Lights, and some half-eaten sandwiches.

On the porch a boerboel sleeps in the shade. I hear the tuk-tuk of the Kreepy Krauly in the pool. I gaze in horror at the photographs in the police files. Such an orderly administration of cruelty.

"Bongani Mfeka became my client in 1996," Piet says. "Client". That is how Piet impassively refers to his serial killers. He plays mind games with them, becomes their confidant, their friend. All along he has only one thing in mind: to put them behind bars for as long as possible.

"Bongani had an excellent command of English. He was highly intelligent, but after completing standard eight, he was forced to go and work on the mines in Randfontein. There was no money for further studies. He had the potential to go further but not the opportunity. It frustrated him. He never got married, and always returned to his parents' home for holidays."

Mfeka's arrest was a bit of a coincidence, a stroke of luck, really.

While he had been raping a woman in Kranskop, his victim had fought back ferociously and bitten his hand. In fact, she had actually bitten a piece of his hand off. Then she had managed to escape and had run away. A taxi had stopped for the naked, screaming woman who was running down the road and the driver had taken her to the police station.

When the woman mentioned in her statement that she had bitten off a piece of her attacker's hand, the local detective had immediately phoned the Kranskop clinic and had asked them to alert him should a man walk in with any kind of hand injury.

And so it was that, on 8 September 1996, the thirty-two-year-old Mfeka was arrested at the local clinic.

The provincial head office in Durban then informed Brixton Murder and Robbery that there was something strange about their new rape suspect. He flatly refused to say a single word.

This caught the interrogators' attention. Had Mfeka talked, he would have been just another rapist making a confession. He would have slipped through the police's net, been sentenced for a single misdemeanour, imprisoned and, in due course, set free. But Mfeka chose to keep quiet, thereby focusing undue attention on himself.

Piet shakes his head, still amazed at the role coincidence can play in bringing criminals to book.

Piet went to Kranskop. At the time he had been baffled by a spate of murders in the Nasrec area, south of Johannesburg. Perhaps there was a connection, perhaps this was his man, Piet hoped. As always, he was keen to find a link between cases that had no apparent connection. He stored one more thing in the filing system between his ears: his colleagues at the charge office had also mentioned that there were a number of unsolved murders at Kranskop.

When Piet shook Mfeka's hand – he made a point of greeting every suspect with a shake of the hand, quite deliberately – he took note of the man's lack of aggression. The man seemed neat and polite.

Before they left Kranskop, Piet bought Mfeka a loaf of bread and a Coke, warning him not to make any mess in his car. Piet didn't usually allow anyone to eat in his car, but Mfeka, Piet had noticed, was exceptionally fastidious. He played upon this character trait to make conversation, to try to win the man's trust.

When they stopped at Van Reenen's Pass, Piet continued with this tactic. He invited Mfeka to sit with them, having made a decision not to treat him like a common criminal. In one of the dockets there's a photograph of Mfeka sitting at the fireside, a shy smile on his face and a can of Coke in his hand.

In this friendly atmosphere, Piet got Mfeka to confess.

"It's a strange thing. I've experienced it so many times – you talk to someone about a specific crime and out of the blue he'll ask for something like a glass of water. Then you know: the man wants to confess about other crimes as well.

"Bongani confessed to one murder after another around the fire. I could see he was remorseful. He became quite emotional as he spoke."

In one of the case dockets, Mfeka made the following statement

Bongani Mfeka pointing out a crime scene.

Mfeka with Piet's colleague Willem Steyn.

to Piet: "You men have been involved in the investigation for only a short time and you already know everything about me. The other policemen have been investigating me for months on end and they still know sweet nothing. It is clear that you are interested in your jobs and know what you are doing."

Later, back at Brixton, Piet phoned around to hear whether Mfeka's confessions could be connected with any open murder dockets between 1994 and 1996.

There were several.

At Welverdiend, near Carletonville, Piet learned, a JE docket had been registered – a judicial enquiry, not a murder. "When I looked at the photos, they showed a naked girl with head injuries, lying on her stomach in the veld … and they had registered a JE! For crying out loud! I thought."

Indeed, one of the murders Bongani confessed to had been at Welverdiend.

Piet shakes his head.

Later, Mfeka pointed out the crime scenes in the company of an independent officer and an interpreter. This is normal procedure, to prevent allegations of undue influencing. It's of utmost importance, Piet stresses. Always keep your case watertight. Pay attention to detail. Do everything according to procedure.

"That's where many guys go wrong nowadays," Piet explains. "They think they've got the case in the bag. Then they appear in court and, what do you know, there are minor investigative errors and the suspect walks out a free man."

First they went to Welverdiend. The woman Mfeka had murdered there had been living with him. She was quite a bit older, a kind of mother figure. That was the trigger for the murder, Piet suspects. "Was it his way to escape his domineering mother? Had his love for his mother turned into resentment and hatred?"

Mfeka and the woman had decided to move from Welverdiend

to Kranskop and had loaded all their possessions into Mfeka's car. Welverdiend had scarcely disappeared from sight in the rear-view mirror when Mfeka had decided, on impulse, to kill her. He did so right there at the side of the road, and then continued to Kranskop alone, with the woman's possessions still in his car. He later pointed out to Piet and his men some of the items, such as a TV antenna and a pile of her shoes.

Mfeka also confessed to killing a child at the roadside near Vrede in the Free State, while he was en route to KwaZulu-Natal. After an inquiry Piet learned from the police that they had picked up the body of a child not far from the highway. Then he knew. Mfeka's confessions were not idle fireside talk.

Mfeka told Piet that he had given the schoolgirl a lift. "Then he lost it. He raped and killed her," Piet tells me.

At Kranskop, Mfeka pointed out six more murder scenes. All that remained of one body, Piet recalls, were scraps of clothing, a skull, and a few ribs and teeth. Nothing more. The parents of the victim, Zulu people who lived in a hut, identified her from the scraps of clothing. They were grateful that her remains had been found, and that the killer had been caught. It gave them closure.

Confessing and returning to the crime scenes apparently gave closure to Mfeka as well. "He was calm, relieved to be able to confess and point out where he had committed the murders," Piet remembers. "He seemed to be clearing his conscience."

With the exception of the murders at Vrede and Welverdiend, all the murders took place near Mfeka's home in Kranskop. Piet knew that this tendency was fairly typical, according to the research of Canadian serial-killer expert Dr Kim Rossmo. Dr Rossmo had found that most serial killings took place near the killers' homes. Serial killers seem to feel more in control in familiar surroundings.

When Mfeka came home from the mine on holiday, he killed in Kranskop. One of his victims had even paid him a visit at his parents' home and they had had sex in his bedroom.

The Kranskop taxi rank was his hunting ground. He would strike up a conversation with a girl during a taxi ride and claim that he could find work for her on a farm. Then he would walk into the veld with her, under the pretext that they were on their way to the farm.

He would order his victim to undress. She would be told to kneel on the ground, and then to lie down on her stomach, thereby assuming a subordinate position. Then Mfeka would simultaneously rape and strangle her.

Mfeka committed eight murders in this manner. Four of the bodies were found within walking distance of his parents' home. In his room, the detectives found women's clothing, a purse and Mfeka's diary. The diary contained a list of his victims' names, with the date and exact time that each one had been murdered.

After the braai at Van Reenen's Pass, a unique friendship developed between Piet and Mfeka.

Piet reeled him in gradually. When he asked for solitary confinement because he didn't want to associate with the other dirty prisoners, his request was granted. When he asked for a Bible, Piet brought him a Zulu Bible.

"He would talk to no other detective. I became a father figure to him."

Then Mfeka came with a strange request: he asked to clean Piet's office. And please, asked Mfeka, bring your shoes along, and I'll clean them for you. And your car.

Every subsequent Saturday morning, Piet made a special trip to Brixton for the cleaning session. For two hours Mfeka would clean and vacuum Piet's large office from top to bottom, with Piet patiently waiting for him to finish.

"For Mfeka it was more than just cleaning. It was cleansing."

Piet would confront him about his deeds in an almost fatherly fashion, always speaking calmly, without aggression, without judgment. It was a rare, almost delicate relationship between prisoner and prosecutor.

When Mfeka told Piet that he missed his mother, one weekend Piet undertook the eight-hour drive to Kranskop and back with his prisoner.

"They embraced for a long time. I waited in the car for an hour and a half so that they could talk."

Mfeka's father did not even come out of the house to greet his son.

In the long hours they spent on the road, during the months before his trial began, Mfeka told Piet why he had killed. And how he had killed.

"Mfeka had a thing about dresses. He said it excited him when a woman wore a dress, and that he struggled to control himself. It was as if the devil took possession of him. He killed his victims when they put up a fight, or sometimes merely so that they would not be able to identify him later."

Apart from the woman who had bitten Mfeka's hand and escaped, only two other women had ever got away. Somehow their tears and pleading got through to Mfeka. Both had promised not to lay charges against him. Maybe that had been their salvation.

"A woman in a similar situation should play along," Piet advises. "Be as nice as possible. It might save your life. Except, of course, when your path happens to cross that of a psychopath. Then it's tickets."

Piet says he can identify a psychopath a mile off. The personality disorders, the strange triggers that make them act they way they do, the lack of emotion. Mfeka may have had some serious psychological disorders, but he was no psychopath, Piet reckons.

After he had spent a year in detention, Mfeka's trial finally began. Piet was ready, his court files in perfect order. Just before the court proceedings were to begin, the advocate for the defence came in search of Piet: "My client wants to see you. Alone," he said.

"I went to Bongani's cell in the High Court building. He was glad to see me. Out of the blue he asked me to testify on his behalf. Me – the one who was charging him …

"I said: 'But I'm testifying against you, Bongani.'

"Bongani replied: 'Tell the court the truth. Please, tell them what I told you: that I can't help myself. I'll kill again. They must never set me free.'

"And that's what I testified …" Piet says softly. "It was the first time anything like that had ever happened to me. Bongani apologised in court. What a rare phenomenon – a serial killer with a conscience."

The sinister feeling he sometimes experiences in the presence of a serial killer was almost completely absent in Mfeka's case. "If I'd met Bongani under other circumstances, I would have thought him to be a bank teller or an office clerk."

What went wrong with Mfeka, Piet surmises, was his relationship with his mother. She intimidated and suffocated him. He developed a mania about women who resembled his mother: slim women who wore dresses. Always slender, never overweight – like his mother.

In a way, it was his mother he killed. Time after time.

His father's cold indifference might suggest that he would rather have wanted to murder men, but this was not the case. While he craved his father's attention, he wanted to free himself from his overbearing mother. Perhaps he had hoped that a murder would make his father sit up, take notice of the boy in whom he had never shown any interest.

But here Mfeka failed. Again. His father did not attend the trial. Only his mother sat in court, faithfully and stoically. When the judge handed down the sentence, Mfeka was visibly satisfied. His mother stared straight ahead. Mfeka was sent to prison in Pietermaritzburg for 112 years: eight life sentences for murder, two life sentences for rape.

After the sentencing, Mfeka asked that Piet come to his cell one last time. He wanted to say goodbye. He asked Piet to remain in contact with him, but they have talked on the phone only once since that day. Other cases, other serial killings, have claimed Piet's time and attention.

Piet draws on his cigarette behind the flame of his lighter. He draws the smoke deep into his lungs and sits in silence for a moment before exhaling it in a lazy swirl.

"Of course one cannot forgive Bongani Mfeka for his cruel deeds. All the same … "

All the same …

At the time of Mfeka's sentencing, Piet was up to his ears in another serial-killer investigation. Although he didn't know it at the time, he had embarked on what would become the longest pursuit of his career.

Piet's path had crossed with one of South Africa's most notorious serial killers ever, one who would make Bongani Mfeka look like an angel of mercy. His name was Lazarus Mazingane.

A TAXI RIDE TO DEATH

He wraps the cord around his victim's neck.

Tighter, ever tighter.

That's the stimulus, the satisfaction. Not the sex. The sex is a bonus. No, it's the feeling of complete control when he pulls the cord as tight as possible.

His victim fights until she loses consciousness, but he carries on strangling her to make sure she's dead. It can take up to four minutes.

He keeps it up until the bloodvessels in the eyes pop, the tongue turns purple. The pressure usually causes blood to gush from the nose and mouth. It's an implosion, almost, as oxygen fails to reach the brain.

Lazarus Mazingane's distinguishing mark is the knot. In the nether world of serial killers, it's his trademark.

A double loop, pulled tightly across the throat – the Mazingane knot.

It is exactly the same, every time: the woman's hands are tied behind her back so that she can't put up much of a struggle. He turns her on her back, rapes and strangles her and then turns her back onto her stomach, before tying the ankles together.

Every time. The knot, the turning of the victim – his own special routine.

The rhythm of a kill.

It's quiet. For minutes we just sit. Piet's mind is far away. Outside there's the dim sound of a dove cooing.

A grave sound.

"There was a tendency of bodies in the Nasrec area," Piet begins.

Police lingo.

His eyes are unfathomable. He blows smoke into the air. Any moment now the small cough will follow.

They were young women, all of them. Raped and strangled near the Nasrec exhibition grounds on a tract of no-man's-land beside the N1, south of Johannesburg.

For fifteen months – since 1995 – no detective could make any headway with the investigation. While the bodies were piling up – on some days two or three bodies would be found – the dockets were ineptly being shuffled between police units.

Months dragged by before the penny dropped: an extremely active serial killer was on the prowl.

Then came the turning point. On 6 May 1996, just like every other morning, fourteen-year-old Prudence Miller took a taxi to Parktown Girls' High School.

Her mother probably had to scrimp and save to send the clever, vivacious teenager all the way from Naturena to this particular school, Piet surmises.

"I suppose Prudence was to have the opportunities her own mother had never had."

In the mornings, Prudence said goodbye to her mother at their flat and waited for the taxi in front of the prison across the road.

But that morning Prudence did not arrive at school. Her battered body was later found near the intersection of Sport and Nasrec Roads. She had been brutally raped and strangled.

There was a public outcry against young Prudence's gruesome demise. It's always the case, Piet nods, when children are murdered – people are up in arms; they want action.

The pressure on the police to do something about the "tendency of bodies" increased. Later that month the top brass decided that Byleveld should take over the case. It was time for damage control.

After Piet's success with the Wessels and Havenga case, he had been tasked by the National Commissioner to investigate serial killings in South Africa in 1994.

He was pleased as punch. "Serial cases challenge the hell out of me. There's something to be said for the satisfaction of connecting someone not only with one case but with several others, and not only in one place but all over the country. And then to piece together all the clues, all the bits of information."

In 1995, Piet was promoted to lieutenant – and then to captain, after the ranks in the police had been changed. Rank by rank, he was on his way to the top.

Piet rubs his forefinger against the bridge of his nose. It's a habit that I have become familiar with: he does it when he gets irritated.

It's New Year's Eve, 2007. Piet doesn't do New Year's Eve. But later that afternoon, after he has dropped me at the airport, he has to join friends for a New Year's party. Esmie is already there. She has phoned five times to ask when he will be finished. And to remind him to bring her sandals. She phones again. He'll remember the sandals? He answers politely, formally. His voice gives nothing away but his impatience shows on his face as he slams the cellphone down, gets up and walks to the fridge for another beer.

He sits down again. Rubs his nose. Focuses on Nasrec.

"It was an incredibly long investigation before I caught this client. Four years. In four years a lot of people can die."

Under a barrage of media pressure, Commissioner George Fivaz held a special press conference to announce that Piet was taking over the investigation. Fivaz even undertook a chopper flight over the murder scenes to bring himself up to speed. With great fanfare, a team of fourteen detectives was assigned to Piet. Six months later

The scene where Prudence Miller was found.

The Mazingane knot.

all fourteen were quietly deployed elsewhere. And, once again, it was up to Piet, Lucky Ramaboea, Ronnie Magina and Moosa Shezi.

Ten Nasrec murder dockets landed on Piet's desk in one go. He almost drowned in paperwork, he remembers. Sometimes he didn't go to bed for four, five days, pumping himself full of Grandpa and Coke to stay awake.

"You should try it. Really. It works," he says.

Piet took over a shaky case. And Fivaz wanted results. Quickly.

From the beginning, mistakes had been made. Important clues found at the murder scenes had never been sent away for forensic analysis. There were gaps in the investigations. It was a nightmare. To crown it all, the detectives had made information freely available to the media. Details about every scene, even maps of the surrounding areas, had been published.

"I knew we had problems that were going to complicate my investigation. The serial killer knew exactly what was going on."

Piet's suspicions were later confirmed by the killer himself. He had indeed followed the initial police investigation on TV and in the papers, until Piet took over the case and forbade any further release of information. The information in the press had enabled the killer to play cat and mouse with the police. He changed his modus operandi after every newspaper report, he had told Piet with a smirk. Clever.

"That's why it's such a kick-ass feeling to hunt serial killers," says Piet, cutting off Esmie's umpteenth call without hesitation. Click.

"Serial killers are cunning, damned intelligent; they push any detective to his limits."

Masters of crime. Both murderer and detective.

When he paged through the dockets for the first time, Piet noticed the similarities between the victims. They were all personable and well groomed and, interestingly, most were wearing nail polish. Brightly coloured nail polish, to be precise, he remembers. Oh yes, and all but one of them had been wearing a dress.

Dresses and nail polish were on the murderer's checklist, in other words.

Another of Piet's observations was confirmed by the victims' families during subsequent interviews. It was like a sad refrain: she left for work in the morning, and she never came home.

Pauline Mahlangu's son was seven when his mother disappeared in Ormonde on 24 March 1996. The boy kept repeating, "My mommy took a taxi to the city, I don't know when she's coming back," *The Star* reported at the time. He's still waiting.

Piet began to wonder: could it have something to do with the victims' mode of transport? Could the killer be a taxi driver?

Studying the photos in the dockets, he continued to build a clearer picture of the serial killer.

We page through the dockets together. These aren't crime scenes, they're battlefields, I think to myself.

One victim's legs and arms are twisted and tucked underneath her; and her head has been bashed in. The murder weapon has been tossed beside the body: a blood-smeared iron bar. Shoes and pieces of clothing lie scattered. Some of the bodies are covered with wounds sustained when the killer cut off the victims' under-clothing with a knife.

Look, Piet points out, some are wearing only one shoe, while the other shoe is placed very deliberately next to the body. Another distinguishing trademark of the killer.

They were all strangled – with the straps of their handbags, panties or their belts. The cord was wrapped around the neck a few times, with the knot exactly at the centre of the throat.

Piet searched worldwide for an expert who could explain the psychology that might lie behind that knot. "Someone had to unravel it for me, if you'll excuse the pun," he says. The only expert he could find lived in America, and it was much too expensive for the police to bring the person over here.

The bodies were spread over a wide area: Nasrec, Naturena, Soweto and Southgate in the south and south-west of Johannesburg, Alexandra and Aeroton in the north-east, and Vosloorus in the East Rand, near Boksburg. Still, there was no doubt that it was the work of the same killer. The forensic team took DNA samples from seven victims. They all matched.

One night, when Piet was once again unable to sleep, he paced around his small garden, musing: what if a number of victims had managed to escape from the serial killer's claws? What if the previous team of investigators had missed this?

The next morning he phoned around to hear if any rapes had been reported in the areas where the killings had taken place.

"And what did I find? Six dockets. Even the circumstances were almost identical. And bloody hell, it was a taxi driver!"

The rape victims had all been presentable, neatly dressed, fitting the profile. Piet paid each of them a visit. They refused to talk to anyone but Piet. "They told me everything," he says, rather smugly. "Perhaps they were just glad that someone was finally doing something about the matter."

All six women described the rapist as a short, slender, neat man in his twenties. A Sotho with a soft voice. His kombi was neat as a pin. A pair of women's panties hung from the rear-view mirror. While he was driving, he played music. A real Romeo.

He selected his prey carefully. It was not just a random choice; our Romeo waited craftily for the right candidate.

In the mornings he would drive his prey to the city and in the afternoons he would take her back home. This would go on for a while – until the afternoon of the murder. Then he would make a detour and drive his victim into the veld. Once he had found a quiet place, he would throw her out of the kombi and walk behind her until he ordered her to lie down on her stomach. If she resisted, he would pull out a knife and threaten her. Then he would rape her.

Just as Piet thought he was hot on the trail of the killer, a new tendency emerged in the Nasrec area. Piet had another serious spate of crimes to investigate. Cars were being hijacked on the highway.

In broad daylight, on roads where hundreds of cars swept past, large rocks were being placed in the middle of the road during a quieter moment. The next approaching car would drive over the rocks and burst a tyre. A man would approach, and offer to help … then all hell would break loose.

"Several people were hijacked and murdered like that. Afterwards, the hijacker would coolly drive away in the car."

In June 1996, after a Sunday afternoon outing to Hartebeespoort Dam, a young married couple drove over some rocks with their bakkie.

They had scarcely come to a stop under a bridge when a man appeared and offered to help. He pulled out a weapon and ordered the husband to move over. He made the wife sit on her husband's lap, while their baby remained in the car seat in the back.

The man drove into the veld, pulled the couple out of the vehicle, forced the man to his knees, and made him watch as he raped his wife while the baby cried hysterically.

The woman's desperate pleas must have struck a chord with the rapist because, out of nowhere, he felt an ounce of mercy. He let the young family go. But he left something behind, something that would bring him ever closer to a prison cell: his semen, his DNA.

Then came another breakthrough. Forensics determined that the DNA of the attacker corresponded with that of the taxi serial killer. It was almost too good to be true – the same killer was using completely different methods. It could be a first in the annals of serial killings, Piet realised: one serial killer with several modi operandi.

"Things were heading in a bizarre direction! First he raped. Then he raped and killed. Then he moved on to hijacking and, if the opportunity arose, he raped and killed the victims."

The hijacker, the couple later told Piet, had been excessively aggressive. He had threatened to kill them if they should go to the police. After he had raped the woman, he had taken the baby out of the vehicle and casually driven away. The helpless family was later found at the roadside and taken to the nearest police station.

Piet says the man blamed himself for not being able to protect his wife. They also told him that they had seen another man standing some distance from the bakkie. Did the serial killer have an accomplice?

This attack, however, was just a finger exercise in terms of cruelty. It was the unfortunate Aspelings who endured the full horror of the Nasrec serial killer's violence.

On 24 July 1997, Gert Aspeling (66) and his wife, Elsie (then 62), an invalid, were driving on the N12 highway. On the outskirts of Johannesburg, near Soweto, close to the old Potchefstroom turn-off, rocks placed in the road damaged a tyre of the Aspelings' Mazda. They were forced to stop.

The hijacker pounced. Gert was reluctant to hand over his keys and was shot in cold blood. The hijacker left his body at the road-side and drove away with the shocked Elsie.

At Eikenhof, a little further ahead, he drove into a maize field. He pulled the sheepskin seat covers off, threw them on the ground and threw Elsie on top of them. Before he could rape her, her pleas convinced him to leave her alone. He left her there, got into the Mazda, drove to a pawn shop and sold her wheelchair for a few rand.

All through that night and the next scorching day, Elsie lay help-less in the maize field, knowing that her husband's body was lying somewhere at the roadside.

Twenty hours later a tractor driver heard her frantic cries. She was in bad shape, seriously dehydrated. Later, when Piet talked to her, she was still so traumatised that she couldn't tell him exactly what had happened. Piet gave her his word that he would catch her husband's killer.

After Gert's death, Elsie's life fell apart. Not only had she lost her husband, who had also been her carer, but she now had no transport. Ultimately she was forced to move into an assisted-care facility.

"Sometimes when I'm in the area, I pop in to have coffee with her," Piet says, his voice filled with compassion.

For four years the Nasrec monster eluded Piet. Every time he heard about yet another murder, Piet was beside himself. He could not accept it. He felt that he had failed the victims; he saw it as a direct indictment against his skills as a detective.

"You concentrate on one profile, only to discover that the killer has changed his modus operandi. In other countries, serial killers tend to follow the same modus operandi for each murder, but here they use different methods and operate in different areas. It's a feature peculiar to South African serial killings. I don't know why."

Piet was overworked. At one point he was involved simultaneously in no fewer than four serial-killing investigations: Nasrec, Kranskop, Wemmer Pan and the hammer murders. He had to use his inhaler more and more frequently to counteract the three packets of cigarettes he smoked per day. Eventually an oxygen cylinder became a fixture in his office.

He hadn't been on holiday for seven years. "How could I go on holiday? Serial killers don't take leave," he says gruffly.

The situation was consuming him. When he received an award in 1988 as the best serial-killing investigator in South Africa, he was elated. But that evening he paced up and down in his home, worrying. He got back into his car and went in search of the Nasrec murderer.

For a detective, a serial killer is the most difficult "client" to remain objective about, Piet says. "Especially if you can't manage to catch him, and he keeps on killing. You know you could be phoned at any moment to be told that another body has been discovered. With every new murder you feel guilty, as if you could have prevented it."

A bitter expression around his mouth. Feeling helpless is hell.

In 2000, by a bizarre coincidence, an attorney's wife drove into a rock ambush on the highway. While she was phoning a friend for help, she was overpowered and raped. She managed to get away, however, and it was with her assistance that the perpetrator was later arrested. He pleaded guilty and was sentenced to thirty-five years' imprisonment for rape with aggravating circumstances.

Piet was unaware of this incident. For some unknown administrative reason, he only heard of the case some months later. He was furious. While he was battling day and night to catch a serial killer, someone who neatly fitted the profile had been imprisoned and he had not been notified. "When I heard about it, I jumped into my car and drove to the forensic laboratory in Pretoria. Fortunately, some of the prisoner's DNA was available. We compared it with the DNA from my cases – the bloody same! His game was up."

At last Piet could attach a name to his serial killer: Lazarus Tshidiso Mazingane (27) from Diepkloof, Soweto.

He coughs. Coincidence, yes, he nods. It often plays a role. But it's usually ninety-nine per cent donkey work and one per cent coincidence. You have to be prepared to put in all those hours of donkey work. Piet was.

With Mazingane safely behind bars, Piet could use his time to carefully prepare the charges against him.

But first he wanted to know: Who is Lazarus Tshidiso Mazingane?

So Piet Byleveld picked up the scent. He went back to Mazingane's beginnings, to the killer's first cry in the Kroonstad prison, where he had been born in 1973. His mother, Meisie, had been serving a five-year sentence for prostitution and dealing in dagga. His first memory had been of a prison cell. It was a humiliation for which he would never forgive his mother.

"While Bongani Mfeka had buried his hatred for his mother deep inside, Lazarus openly cursed his mother."

His mother later got married, became an alcoholic and continued to deal in dagga. Lazarus was raised by his grandmother in Brits, before attending Diepkloof High School. In Vosloorus, where she was living at the time, Meisie later told Piet that she knew that her son hated her. When she spoke about him, Piet remembers, she was totally indifferent. "You could see there was not an ounce of maternal love."

Deprived of the love of a mother, born in prison – the seed for misogyny had been sown early in what became a lonely, ill-fated life.

It was with Nompi that Mazingane found love. Nompi with the gentle eyes, his school friend from Diepkloof, whom he later married. But her love was not enough to wipe out his hatred and anger.

He abused Nompi appallingly, both physically and emotionally. He would tie her to the bed and have sex with other women while she was forced to watch helplessly.

After he had shot at her during one of his regular bouts of fury, Nompi fled to her parents' home and laid a charge against him. He later kidnapped her, brutally assaulted her, drove back to her parents' home and threw her out of his taxi, leaving her in an unconscious heap on the pavement. He shouted at her mother: "Take back your fucking bitch."

Then he stormed into the house and fired wildly at Nompi's parents. Fortunately, her mother, a strong woman, managed to drive him away. Nompi refused to lay another charge against her husband. "But later she was a fantastic witness in court. She described in detail how cruel he was. She still feared him intensely. In the courtroom she wouldn't come near him, wouldn't even look at him."

Finally Piet decided he knew enough. It was time to meet Lazarus Mazingane. Time to look in the eye the man who had managed to evade him so effortlessly for four long years.

Time to rev it up a little.

"I knew enough about him by then to realise I had better be careful. At Diepkloof Prison I booked him out, putting him in cuffs and shackles so that he would understand: I control you, pal, you don't control me. It was the only language he understood.

"When I told him who I was, he was instantly aggressive. On the way to Brixton, he kept asking: 'Why are we going to Murder and Robbery? I'm serving my sentence, what do you want from me?'"

All the way there, Piet ignored him. When they drove through the gates, Mazingane went crazy. They had to use force to get him into a cell. "He swore at me, using every expletive in the book."

When he realised Piet was on his case, he knew he was in for big trouble, Mazingane later admitted.

"Remember, I've put a lot of criminals behind bars, and I'm a topic of discussion there. I can walk into any jail right now and you won't believe how many Piet Specials will greet me."

Piet left Mazingane to stew in his Brixton cell for a few days. Mazingane kept asking to see Piet, but all he got was a typical reply: "I'll talk to you when I feel like it."

Coolly, Piet played him.

A few days later, at about two in the morning, the constables phoned Piet. Mazingane had lost his marbles, had defecated in his food and started throwing it at the guys in the charge office.

"I rushed through to Brixton, furious. The audacity! I hosed him down with a garden hose and after a while he calmed down."

It was only their second meeting, but that night Mazingane got to see a different side of Piet Byleveld. "I didn't assault him; it's not my style. I just made him understand: we're not going to take your shit. You don't get to call the shots.

"I have respect for people, it's in my nature, but I won't be messed around. Not after all the years at Murder and Robbery."

After that dramatic night, Piet introduced his tenderising routine. At first he made no mention of the charges against Mazingane, but worked with him as an individual, focusing on Mazingane himself. When he discovered that Mazingane loved soccer, Piet brought him the *Sowetan* each morning, so that he could follow the results. But Piet never mentioned soccer himself. It was leverage he would only use later.

During their third meeting, Piet resorted to his old trick – the one that always created a bond between him and the serial killer. He booked Mazingane out of jail and, accompanied by Lucky Ramaboea and Ronnie Magina, drove Mazingane to Brits to visit his grandmother.

His father was also there, but Mazingane didn't know that.

Before they left, Piet bought Mazingane a pie, a cooldrink and a Bar-One at Tasty's. Piet had found out that Bar-One was his favourite chocolate bar, but, again, it was information he was reserving for later.

In the car, they talked about soccer. Piet knew it would calm Mazingane down, make him relax.

Somewhere near Hartebeespoort Dam the conversation took a different turn.

"Do you like girls?" Piet began.

"Yes, I dig them big-time."

"You have many girlfriends?"

"Yes."

"Mmm, I found that out."

Mazingane was silent for a while. Piet knew he had touched a nerve. The conversation continued.

"What kind of sport do you like?"

"Soccer."

Piet: "Mmm. I know you do."

Mazingane was silent. Piet wanted him to realise: I know all about you.

Piet: "There's something I want to tell you: I know you were born in prison."

And then Mazingane lost it. Furious, he cursed his mother, shouting: "She fucked up my life!"

When Piet describes the vehemence of Mazingane's outburst, it is as though the man's fury is palpable even here in this garden flat, between Piet and me.

"One almost feels sorry for Lazarus Mazingane," I venture.

Piet's head jerks up in irritation. "No," he says so loudly that the boerboel at our feet looks up, startled.

"To be born in prison …"

"Of course it sucks to be born in prison, but it didn't give him the right to do what he did. Think about the victims. Think. About. The. Victims. I don't judge, but I don't have empathy with murderers. They don't have to kill, they always have a choice."

Then Piet returns to the conversation he had with Mazingane during their trip to Brits. "I know you had a taxi," said Piet. "But tell me, Lazarus, why were there panties in your kombi?"

Mazingane said nothing for a while. Then he grinned. "I'm crazy about women's underclothes."

Piet gave Lucky's shoulder a pat. His colleagues began to laugh and looked at him. "We knew each other so well; they knew we were striking the right notes now, and that sooner or later this man was going to co-operate."

In the township at Brits, Mazingane was more or less the last person his father was expecting to see. Piet had not let the father know in advance – he wanted to see how they would both react.

"It was no happy encounter."

Mazingane refused to talk to his father. Piet went into the house

to get a statement from the father. He was following up information that Mazingane had once arrived there in a Ford Escort that
had been seized in a hijacking. The father confirmed it.

"The grandmother was hostile. You could see she cared for
Lazarus. It obviously upset her to see him in the back of the police
car. They were respectable people, though. The house was clean."

After the trip to Brits, Piet and Mazingane began to get along a
little better. Piet gave him a radio so that he could listen to soccer
broadcasts in his cell – on condition that he behaved.

After that, Mazingane phoned Piet regularly on Saturday mornings when the batteries of his radio were flat. Piet always delivered
the new ones personally. In time, their relationship became cordial
and Mazingane began to co-operate.

Then, barely six months into the new millennium, Lazarus
Mazingane and Piet Byleveld both had significant events happen
in their lives.

On 9 June 2000, Mazingane was able to lift his seven-year-old
daughter onto his lap and hold her for the very last time in the
world that exists beyond the prison walls. And on the same day
Martiens Byleveld died. Piet lost his father, his hero, his compass.

Four days earlier Piet had his father admitted to the
HF Verwoerd Hospital in Pretoria. Martiens Byleveld had
advanced spinal cancer, and the pain had become unbearable.

Confident that his father was in good hands, Piet decided to take
Mazingane to the Eastern Cape to follow up a lead. Mazingane had
apparently visited a sangoma there and told him certain things. As
it happened, however, they were unable to find the sangoma.

While they were in the Eastern Cape, Piet got word that his
father was dying.

"I drove back immediately, dropped Mazingane at Brixton in the
late evening and went directly to the hospital. While I was walking

down the corridor, I heard a terrible sound, like an animal in pain. It was my father. Fortunately, in a lucid moment, he was able to recognise me. The pain gradually became worse.

"At midnight, I asked the nurses to give him a shot of morphine. After that, he calmed down. At five that morning he was gone.

"It was …" Piet searches for the right words, "hard to handle. My father suffered terribly before he died. No person should die like that …"

For a moment there are tears in the eyes of this hardened cop. Just for a moment.

"At least I was able to say goodbye to my father …"

Just after dawn Piet left his family, got into his car and drove from Pretoria back to Brixton to fetch Mazingane. It was the day on which Mazingane's visit to his little girl had been scheduled. Postponing the visit never even entered Piet's mind. He had given Mazingane his word.

"Work comes first," Martiens Byleveld had drilled into his son years before.

In Pietersburg, Piet left Mazingane alone with his daughter and her mother. When Mazingane later had to take leave of her, he was emotional.

During the journey back to Brixton, Mazingane did not say a word in the car. At Naboomspruit Piet turned off to join his own family in Nylstroom, and his colleagues drove back to Johannesburg with Mazingane.

"When we said goodbye, Lazarus thanked me. All his aggression was gone."

Piet would remember 9 June 2000 as the day his father died; Mazingane would remember it for that special visit to his young daughter.

Although his father's death had come as a big shock to Piet, it didn't even enter his mind that he could take a few days off to mourn. He dealt with his loss by immersing himself in his work.

"Shortly after Lazarus's visit to his daughter I woke up one night and knew: I have to put the pressure on."

Over the next few days Mazingane confessed to one murder after another. "That's how I work. I keep prodding, looking for that weak spot that will catch the suspect off guard, as it were. With Bongani Mfeka it was his mother, though I didn't really focus on it. With Mazingane it was definitely his young daughter."

And his own? What is Piet Byleveld's weak spot?

The question catches him off guard as well. Suddenly he's ill at ease.

"I love children," he says a moment later – the man who doesn't have any children of his own.

By this time Piet had enough forensic evidence to prove that Mazingane was the Nasrec killer: DNA from blood and hair samples (pubic as well as body hair) belonging to Mazingane corresponded with that of hair found on the bodies.

But, as always, Piet wanted his case to be more than watertight. He also wanted confessions and the killer's identification of the various murder scenes. So he sat down at a table with Mazingane for three whole days. "I told him: Lazarus, I've done my bit, and now I expect you to do the same. And I'm not going to stop until you've told me everything. It's show-time."

Piet's interrogation was abrupt and to the point, almost staccato. Did he have a taxi? Yes. Did he transport women in it? Yes. Did he take them into the veld? Yes. Then he raped them? No, they agreed to have sex with him. Don't talk shit, do you mean to tell me that ten, twelve of them all agreed? A long silence. No. Another silence. It's true … he did rape them.

The smaller fish were in the bag – the rape charges. Now for the big ones, the murders. Initially, Mazingane was hesitant. Then Piet focused on Prudence Miller, the young schoolgirl. Forensically, that particular case was already watertight.

Initially he vehemently denied the charge.

Why had he always let her sit in the front passenger seat?

Mazingane grinned: "She was pretty, and her short school uniform turned me on. I would play her nice music while we were driving. She slept with me too."

"No," Piet told him, "now I know you're talking shit, because she was a virgin before you raped her."

Yes, okay, sorry, he did rape and kill her. It was as if the confession had just slipped out.

And immediately Mazingane was furious with himself because he had confessed. He wanted to bite his tongue, Piet could see. Piet went out and bought him a Bar-One. When he returned half an hour later, Mazingane was calm.

Piet then carried on with his questioning. After Prudence Miller's death, someone had phoned her mother and told her he knew where her child was. The caller had asked her to meet him at Nasrec. She had gone, but there had been no one there.

Mazingane confessed: he had been the man on the phone. When he saw Prudence's mother crying on TV, he felt sorry for her. So he phoned. He'd meant it as a tip so that the police would search for the body there.

Piet shakes his head, then tells me, "For some reason he felt sorry for the mother. At the time Lazarus told his wife, Nompi, that he couldn't understand why the police didn't catch the man, because he was obviously going to kill more women."

But back at Brixton, the floodgates had opened. For three days Mazingane talked non-stop. When he grew tired, they took a break. Sometimes Mazingane was aggressive, at other times Piet and he laughed together.

"When he realised that he was trapped on the DNA evidence alone, he opened up completely. It was as if he wanted to share everything with me."

Piet realised with a shudder that he was face to face with a monster.

Today he still wonders: How much did Mazingane really confess? How many more murders were there that the fresh-faced young man had kept secret? How many bleached bones were still lying in a deserted veld somewhere?

"He became so blasé that he would just grab any girl who was walking along the road and kill her."

At one stage, he had developed a taste for little girls. He pointed out places at Orange Farm where he had killed four young girls. One of them, he boasted, he had lured with chocolates.

The state eventually decided not to charge Mazingane with the murders of these children. Despite his confession, the cases were not watertight. Piet went to tell the young victims' parents that their children's killer was probably in jail. He can only hope that the knowledge brought them some measure of peace.

Mazingane supplied Piet with his checklist for the perfect victim:

☑ Young, well bred, in a neat dress.
☑ Preferably a working girl, no prostitutes – he saw himself as superior to them.
☑ Submissive – aggression irritated him. Any opposition would always lead to murder.
☑ Bright nail polish – this was a great stimulus.
☑ High-heeled shoes – just as important. Some of the women had ill-fitting shoes, Mazingane told Piet. They looked clumsy. After a murder he often removed one shoe and placed it neatly beside the body.

These were the triggers that could set Mazingane off. In one instance it had been a nurse's smart blue shoes that had led to her death. He had stalked the poor woman over a long period, often giving her a lift between her home and a hospital in Morningside. After a while he had asked his taxi boss if he could work on Sundays as well, so that he could take her to church. The nurse told her parents about the kind taxi driver who picked her up at home. This "courtship" continued for a few months. Mazingane managed to control himself, until at last he pounced, and raped and murdered her.

In the meantime, the list of victims grew ever longer.

It also emerged that Mazingane's wingman, the one whom the hijacked couple had mentioned, was one Kaiser Motsegwa. He drove around in the taxi with Mazingane, always the onlooker because he was too sick with Aids to take part in the raping.

Mazingane was in complete control of Motsegwa. He threatened to kill him if he talked. Motsegwa was so afraid of him that when he was apprehended and taken into custody, he pleaded not to be locked up in the same police station as Mazingane. He was later found guilty of only one charge: robbery with aggravating circumstances.

Lazarus Mazingane was a classic serial killer, the fifth in the legal history of South Africa. No one in his family or work circle could believe that he was a killing machine. His taxi boss, who lived three houses away from him, was completely taken aback when Piet told him the horrific truth about his employee.

"He was upset at first, then furious, and then afraid the other taxi bosses would blame him. I had to go and tell them that the poor man had had no inkling of Mazingane's true nature."

To his immediate acquaintances and friends Mazingane had seemed like an ordinary kind of guy. He worked during the day, he was part of a social network and had a good circle of friends. Every evening he scrubbed his taxi until it was spotless.

"Ja, but it's that same symbolic washing of the hands again," Piet muses, suddenly philosophical in the final hours of the old year.

We laugh.

Piet's cellphone rings. It's Esmie again. Click, he cuts off the call.

Mazingane's grudge against women had begun at his mother's knee in a prison cell. Like Bongani Mfeka, every woman he humiliated, raped and killed was actually his mother.

Piet, ever inquisitive, was insistent on finding out why Mazingane had tied up poor Nompi and made her watch him having sex with other women. It was her punishment because she had cheated on him, was Mazingane's curt reply, suddenly no longer the serial killer, but the injured husband.

His young daughter and his girlfriend, whom Piet heard about only later, knew only his benevolent side. He showered his girlfriend with gifts of rings and earrings he had looted from his victims. She nearly fainted when she learned that she had shared her bed with a serial killer.

Piet laughs. "She had been, let's say, a bit worried, because the jewellery he kept bringing her always appeared slightly used."

The trial in the Johannesburg High Court lasted nine months. There were an astounding 270 witnesses, all meticulously prepared by Piet. The prosecutors were Advocate Gerrit Roberts (sc) and Advocate Nicolette Bell, with Judge Joop Labuschagne on the bench in Court 4B.

"Mazingane's girlfriend attended the proceedings. Initially she supported him, but when she saw the way things were going, she promptly disappeared."

Mazingane's alcoholic mother, in her unwitting way the catalyst for this orgy of violence, was nowhere to be seen, not even when the verdict was returned.

State pathologist Patricia Klepp painted a horrific picture of the victims' suffering to their friends and relatives, who filled the courtroom to capacity. She gave a graphic description of death by strangulation. After four minutes, irreversible brain damage occurs.

Advocates Nicolette Bell and Gerrit Roberts and Piet with files of evidence against Lazarus Mazingane (top).

OPPOSITE: *Markers showing crime scenes on a photo showed in court.*

Sometimes the circulation back to the body is cut off, which creates pressure and causes the arteries to burst.

Mazingane was described by Judge Labuschagne as an extremely aggressive, arrogant, vague and untruthful witness. There had been no conspiracy against him, he stated emphatically, and Mazingane's allegations that Piet had tortured him were rejected.

On 22 December 2002, in the Johannesburg High Court, the judge and two assessors sentenced Lazarus Tshidiso Mazingane (29) to seventeen life sentences and 781 years in prison. He was found guilty on seventy-four of the seventy-five counts brought against him.

Mazingane stared straight ahead, expressionless, when he was found guilty on more than sixteen counts of murder, five of attempted murder, three of kidnapping, twenty of robbery with aggravating circumstances and twenty-two of rape and the illegal possession of firearms and ammunition.

He looked up only once, straight at the man who had worked for four years to get him in the dock: Piet Byleveld.

Months later, Lazarus phoned Piet. He just wanted to hear whether Piet was okay; he was worried about him …

"Can you believe it!" Piet shakes his head.

After he had spent six years in the Leeuwkop Prison, Mazingane addressed a group of high-school children who were on a visit to the prison: "Many of you don't have mothers and sisters because of people like Lazarus Mazingane. Don't do what I have done. Prison is not a good place to be."

Lazarus Mazingane started his life in prison, and he will end his life in prison. Full circle.

We drive to the airport, not once under the speed limit. Piet has his party to go to, and I have a flight to catch. "Don't forget the sandals," I remind him.

"What-a-bloody-year," Piet sighs as he drives steadily in the right-hand lane. "At least I got to shake Madiba's hand."

Ex-president Mandela had told his assistant, Zelda la Grange: get Piet Byleveld, I want to thank him for his hard work. "I never thought it would happen to an ordinary old cop like me. He told me he was very proud of me …" The asthmatic voice has a tremor in it.

The photograph of Piet with Madiba, signed by the great man himself, has been enlarged and put in a fancy frame. It has an honorary place in his home, covering nearly an entire wall.

I watch Piet's face as his Chev slips out of the police parking spot at the airport. We wave one last time; 2007 is behind us, 2008 lies ahead.

Suddenly he looks very alone.

THE WEMMER PAN KILLER

The yellow Cressida cruises slowly down the dirt road and comes to a halt on the grass beside Wemmer Pan.

It's afternoon; it's quiet; it's secluded. The battered car seats are lowered, clothing that gets in the way is unceremoniously stripped off.

It's high tide for the libido, riding the waves on the Cressida's aged shocks.

The car rocks.

Suddenly, the door is jerked open, the man is pulled out of the car and shot with his own pistol, a 9mm Parabellum Star M30. He falls on his stomach beside the car and lies in a twisted heap in his bright green-and-yellow soccer top, his trousers around his ankles, one arm outstretched, the hand in a supplicating gesture.

Minutes later he is dead.

His life has ended in a climax.

Then it's the woman's turn. She is raped and her head viciously beaten to a pulp. She lies in the winter grass in her blue-and-white polka-dot dress.

In the air lingers the bitter smell of blood and the muskiness of semen.

Later the police knock on a front door in Mayfair. They are the bearers of gruesome tidings. "I'm sorry, ma'am," the detective begins sympathetically, "your husband has been murdered. Together with a woman. We found them at Wemmer Pan ..."

The woman bursts into tears and weeps hysterically in the doorway.

Piet unfolds the Grandpa with practised fingers. His fingers are slender, like those of a pianist.

He clears his throat, opens another docket in that overcrowded mind of his.

"In June 1997 the station commander at Booysens informed me that there was a tendency at Wemmer Pan in the south of Johannesburg. Interestingly, the murders took place only on weekends, somewhere between Friday evening and Sunday afternoon."

Someone's macabre weekend pastime, in other words.

When Piet took over the investigation, about fifteen women had been murdered in the vicinity of Wemmer Pan in a little more than a year – the murderer was clearly very active. Piet knew at once that this was his next serial killer. The hunt was on.

By then, Piet had established a firm reputation as an investigator of serial killings. The media had taken note of him; they were writing about the solemn detective in his immaculate suits, the detective who never threw in the towel.

"Little did I know what was waiting for me," Piet mutters under his breath.

And little did this slight detective know, when he dropped me off at the airport on New Year's Eve 2007, what would be waiting for him during the twelve months to follow.

One morning in May 2008 Piet worked up the courage to tell Esmie that he couldn't live with her any longer and he wanted a divorce. She stared at him, speechless, while he threw a few items of clothing into a travel bag. Later, in an interview with *The Star*, Esmie said she wasn't surprised. She even helped him carry his bags to the bakkie.

When he drove through the gates of the security complex, he felt only one emotion: relief. "I was so relieved that I had finally taken the step, that I was finally on my own, that I no longer had to live with the fear of her next outburst. Because that was terribly hard for me.

"I was only about three blocks away when she phoned, swearing incessantly. Verbal abuse, I'm telling you."

That call, Piet remembers, was the final confirmation he needed that he couldn't stay with Esmie for a moment longer. The sudden certainty comforted him.

He sighs. "Worst was when she would wake me in the small hours, screaming and cursing for no reason at all. I'm sure even the neighbours could hear every damned word."

The last straw was when she started threatening to set Piet's Mercedes and Bantam bakkie alight.

"I was forced to remove the vehicles from the premises," Piet says. Though clearly upset, he still uses the judicial jargon that has become part of his personality. Forced. Remove. Premises.

The Mercedes that had come as part of Piet's remuneration when he was promoted to director in 2007 had become an issue between them, he tells me. Esmie had refused point-blank to drive in the car with him. "She said that when we drove in the Mercedes, I considered myself superior to her because I had become this hot-shot director."

For Esmie, perhaps, the Mercedes became a symbol of her husband's estrangement from her, of the rapid disintegration of their marriage. So she expressed herself in the only way she thought possible: I refuse to drive in it with you. I'm not a part of your fancy new life. You've left me behind. You're riding this wave of success on your own.

"That's sad," I tell Piet.

At first it's as if he doesn't hear me. Then he shakes his head slowly. "There's no love left between us," he says. "I don't hate her, but I despise the things she's done to me."

I glance furtively at Piet. He does seem more relaxed these days, as if there's a huge weight off his mind.

The end of the road for the passengers of the pale-yellow Cressida.

But there's something else.

The moment I saw him waiting for me in front of the airport building, in exactly the same place where we had taken our leave of one another on New Year's Eve a year ago, it was as clear to me as the red-and-white Avis sign on the pavement that something was different about Piet. Very different.

The reason for that difference stood beside him. Tall, blonde, wearing a dress in a soft floral print and a hesitant smile.

"Elize Smit," he told me, introducing her a bit awkwardly.

She left us alone with a plate of snacks in Piet's brand-new home, a townhouse in an upmarket development in Ruimsig, Roodepoort. He moved here in September 2008, after staying with his sister and her family in the same complex for a few months.

As Elize left us, Piet followed her appreciatively with his eyes. Where she fitted in, I wasn't sure. He didn't say.

Piet digs around in a docket and pulls out a photo of a woman. Her turquoise T-shirt is pulled up high. A muti cord, which, according to Zulu tribal custom, was supposed to have protected her, lies uselessly under her pale breasts. Her head is turned away, as if she wants to avert her gaze. Her face is unrecognisably battered.

"She was raped. Then her attacker picked up a large rock and repeatedly threw it onto her face."

That was what Piet's client did to single black women. He was more than a murderer. This was more than a murder.

As is so often the case, Piet explains to me, the murderer seemed to fear that his victims would be able to identify him if their eyes were left open, even after death. In photograph after photograph they lie there, their eyes surreally covered by an item of clothing.

As was Piet's habit, he approached this new murder mystery by applying Byleveld's First Rule of Detection: start with the basics.

"Some investigators run around in circles, looking for evidence.

I sit down calmly and reason things out step by step. Without knowing what the motive was, you can't solve a murder case. Motive is everything."

Then he connects the killings one by one until he has a complete picture.

Piet is not the kind of detective that visits a murder scene only once and then that's it. He is so obsessed with detail that he will hang around a murder scene for days. One particular piece of evidence was found, doing just that.

"A week after the body of one of the Wemmer Pan victims had been removed, I found a Kleenex on the scene that had the DNA of the murderer. One Kleenex, one week later … what are the chances? The wind could have blown it away.

"I'll probably return to the crime scene a thousand times. I'll sleep there. Camp there. Smoke with the locals. The smallest detail – like an old cigarette butt – could be the link to the murderer in the end."

It's his acute ability to observe that counts in his favour, he believes. He can make deductions at the scene, place himself in the murderer's shoes. "I try to find out as much as possible about the victims. What kind of work did they do? What were their movements? Their routine? Look, a victim doesn't just come walking up to a killer. What exactly led to the two of them to be in the same area? Gradually those facts lead me to the murderer's modus operandi."

Every clue slots into place somewhere. As the investigation progresses, Piet works with the individual clues, until the bigger picture emerges.

While Piet's investigation of the Wemmer Pan murders was underway, with a woman being murdered almost every weekend, he was suddenly confronted with a new string of murders, also in the vicinity of Wemmer Pan. This time, however, couples were being brutally murdered among the bushes and trees.

The area was well known as a place where men took their lovers for "clandestine meetings", as Piet puts it. The murderer would overpower the couple while they were having sex.

"Caught in the act, one might say. The poor people didn't know what hit them. He sometimes forced them to have sex while he watched."

Without saying a single word, the murderer shot his male victims cold-bloodedly in the back of the head. He always took a shoe as a trophy. Only one. The women were forced to run up a nearby mine dump while he gave chase, swearing all the while, mostly in Afrikaans, interspersed with his favourite English words: "bitch" and "clitoris".

Piet grins when he sees my expression. "Ja, this client gave them hell."

When they reached the top, the women were forced to undress before he raped them. Those who resisted were promptly killed. Those who begged for their lives were sometimes spared if the killer was feeling magnanimous. To some he even gave the taxi fare that would get them home – R4,50. A hand-out from a killer.

Those who got away described him as small but very strong and extremely aggressive. Some of the women were raped three times.

Piet grins. "He boasted to one of his victims about all the murders he had committed. Then he asked to see her again – he actually tried to date her!"

With the murder of the couple in the yellow Cressida, the killer had come into the possession of a pistol and he'd upgraded his method from bashing in heads to shooting to kill. Head shots, mostly.

Almost every weekend there was an attack. The investigation began to take its toll on Piet. As always, he reproached himself after each murder, and on Saturdays and Sundays he would get into his car and drive endlessly around Wemmer Pan.

"I restricted my observation to during the day, because he never attacked at night."

Frustrated, actually "totally fed up", Piet decided to set up an ambush. He devised a plan. He and colleague Riana Steyn, posing as a pair of lovers, would wait for the murderer on top of the mine dump, in the heart of the murder area, in an unmarked car.

"We sat waiting in that blue Toyota Corolla for eight, nine hours."

"Making out?" I ask.

He laughs huskily. "Heh-heh-heh, no, ma'am, nooooo."

Piet had a gut feeling that they were going to catch the killer that day. That was why they sat there for so long. It was getting dark when they decided to call it a day. Piet was beginning to fear for Riana's safety.

Just as they were pulling away, the men sent word by radio that a man was slowly moving up the mine dump, approaching the car.

"It was too late, too dark already, to stop to try to catch him. The moment had slipped through my fingers. I could have kicked myself. And I knew: tonight someone is going to pay."

Piet alerted his men: There's going to be hell to pay, the murderer is going to take revenge.

His feeling was spot-on, he says wryly.

Months later, in the cells, the murderer told Piet just how furious he had felt when he hadn't managed to get to him. He had known he was a policeman and had wanted to kill him. He was like someone on drugs, high on pure anger. As he later explained to a psychologist: "When I'm angry, I can't even speak, there are no words in my mind."

The attempted ambush changed the way the killer behaved. That night was the first time he attacked at night. What was more, he suddenly moved away from the area in which he had usually operated.

He set off for Langlaagte, and it was there, some time later, that he came across Samuel Moleme and his girlfriend, Catherine Lekwene, lying in each other's arms. He shot and killed Samuel and raped Catherine twice before letting her go. He had shot Samuel so unexpectedly, so fast, that when the victim's body was later discovered, his cap was still on his head.

There was a ZCC (Zion Christian Church) badge, Piet remembers, just above the bloody patch where the bullet had struck him in the heart. He too had had a muti cord around his waist. With this murder, however, the murderer had taken both Samuel's shoes as trophies and, in doing so, deviated from his previous pattern, in which he had taken only one.

Five kilometres further away, in Claremont, he found his next victims having sex in some bushes. He shot Pieter John du Plessis, raped his friend Sara Lenkpane, and shot her as well. The police found Pieter's body in a foetal position next to Sara's. Her blue dress was hiked up to her hips. Both had been shot in the head. Again, the killer had taken both shoes of his male victim.

A kilometre further, his bloody path crossed that of fifteen-year-old Lelanie van Wyk and her boyfriend, Martin Stander (19). They had been on their way home from a nightclub in Delarey where Martin was a disc jockey. At half past eleven that night, people had seen them dancing and having a good time. The couple had allegedly gone behind an industrial building for some "alone time" before Martin planned to take Lelanie home.

The murderer ordered Martin to take off everything except his underpants. This was a strange turn of events – he had never made his male victims undress before. He shot Martin in the head and took his clothes and shoes.

They were his third pair of shoes of the night.

Martin lay on his stomach, his slim, boyish body clad only in red underpants and brown socks. Blood was flowing from his ear.

The killer took the terrified Lelanie some distance away, ordered her to undress, raped her and shot her in the head as well. Around her neck was a delicate chain with a small dolphin and a yin-yang symbol, on her hand the stamp of the club where they had been seen earlier that night.

But the killer's bloody trail did not end there.

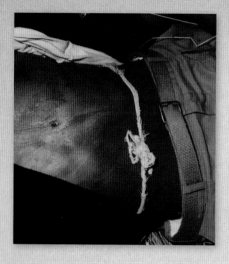

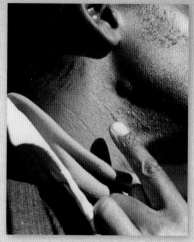

A victim's muti cord.

Michael Mkhize is shot through the neck, but survives.

The murder scene of Lelanie van Wyk and Martin Stander.

The place where Martin Stander was found.

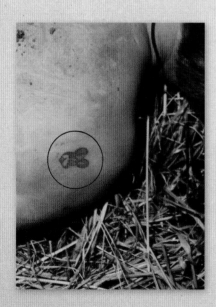

The Minnie Mouse tattoo on Lelanie van Wyk's shoulder was used to identify her.

The nightclub stamp still on Lelanie's hand.

The killer continued in the direction of Main Reef Road, where just before dawn he stopped a taxi in Langlaagte. The taxi driver, Michael Mkhize, took him nearly all the way to his home in Overton before he was forced at gunpoint to drive to an industrial area. He was shot in the neck and left for dead. Miraculously, he survived and was later able to give evidence at the trial. This time the killer took only one shoe.

The new day dawned, scattering shards of light across the mine dumps.

Apart from the taxi driver and the girl that the killer had allowed to go, all the victims of that murderous night lay lined up in the morgue. All five of them.

"The staff had their hands full …" Piet says grimly. "To this day I feel guilty about that night." Piet shakes his head. "I could have prevented it. If only I hadn't driven off, I could have saved the lives of five people."

Details of the murderous orgy were blazoned across the front pages of the papers, and fingers were inevitably pointed. Where were the police? Why couldn't they catch this monster?

Piet started to smoke even more, ate even worse, lay awake even longer at night. His asthma was getting out of control. Eventually he had to start using an oxygen cylinder at night.

"Everyone was on my case. The pressure was tremendous. Everyone, from the media to my seniors, said the same thing: catch this man, and catch him quickly."

After that night of vengeance, it was as if the murderer's thirst for blood could not be quenched. He struck almost every weekend, and had returned to his familiar stomping ground. He continued to shoot his male victims at point-blank range, without saying a word, and always taking one shoe as a trophy.

As obsessed as this man clearly was with killing, just as obsessed was Piet with catching him.

Piet and his team began a relentless observation of the area, spoke to anyone they thought might have seen something, and moved around the area day and night, looking for possible clues. But they found nothing.

Then the next murder would occur. Another missing shoe, and Piet would know: it's him. He'd find the 9mm cartridge cases and he'd know: it's him.

"Hell."

Had such events happened in Europe or America, the police force would undoubtedly have been able to deploy more than a hundred detectives to work on the case. But this was Africa. Here it was just Piet, his Benson & Hedges and his troika of helpers.

An elderly Portuguese man, Gerhard Lavoo, had the habit of riding his bike for exercise every afternoon on a path through the trees beside Wemmer Pan.

"The murderer waited for him, casually shot him in the back as he was riding by and took his bike. Just like that." Piet shakes his head.

"The cartridge cases found at the scene looked as if they had been fired from the weapon used by the Wemmer Pan serial killer. I realised we were dealing with a superkiller, who kept changing his modus operandi.

"I mean – shooting and killing an old man for a bicycle! The entire sexual motive went down the chute."

To confound the profile even more, the murderer would randomly spare his victims' lives. At the La Rochelle soccer field adjacent to Wemmer Pan, he had allowed a couple to leave after he had wounded the man and raped the woman twice. This was the couple that was later able to identify him from a line-up.

"The semen was also linked positively to him," says Piet. "In a way, his semen was also the seed of his downfall." He gives a wheezy laugh. "Time and again it linked him to a rape."

But still the killer remained at large, and the number of victims continued to rise.

On 19 December 1997, an excited couple's outing to the circus ended in tragedy. Bongani Khama, a security guard, and his girlfriend, Ntombifuthi, were on their way to the circus in Regent's Park. They were walking through a park when Khama heard a shot being fired. At first he thought it was a firecracker but then he felt a warm sensation in his back and an acute burning pain. He fell to the ground.

The murderer squatted beside him and in broken Zulu asked for money. Khama gave him the R180 he had for their circus tickets, while he kept praying: "God, what is going to happen to me? What is going to happen to my family? Spare me, please."

Just before he lost consciousness, the killer told him that his girlfriend was going to die.

She did.

But Bongani's prayers for his own survival were answered.

In Piet's townhouse, the telephone rings. He frowns. It's Esmie. No, he can't come to see what's wrong with the lights today, he tells her firmly. No, he can't come tomorrow either, he's busy. She continues talking, the pitch of her voice rising. He answers curtly. After a while I hear her voice become even shriller. He cuts her off, and looks at me.

"Where were we? Oh yes, and then the breakthrough came at Wemmer Pan. Out of the blue."

Someone from the area, a vigilant member of the public, became suspicious of a man who was hanging around a hotel without actually drinking or eating there. He gave the police a description and said that he thought the man might be having a relationship with a certain woman there.

The description matched the picture that, from the accounts given by survivors, Piet had by then formed in his mind: a small, thin man, usually clad in neat green trousers and a grey jersey with the faded impression of a face on it.

"That was when things began to develop. I found out the girl-friend was Angelina Tlapane, and she worked at a dog parlour."

Early on the morning of 23 December 1997, Piet and his partners began their surveillance of Tlapane. They followed her. At about eleven o'clock, she got into a taxi and travelled towards Jeppe. Near the railway station she got out and waited on the corner of John Page and Pine Road.

A small man clad in green trousers and a grey jersey came saun-tering along. Piet knew instantly: this was his man.

The team pounced, arresting the man on the spot. In his right trouser pocket they found a cartridge. "I read him his rights and told him he was suspected of murder and rape. You can't even begin to imagine what pleasure I got from that."

The man didn't say a word.

Six months. That was how long it had taken Piet to catch one of South Africa's cruellest serial killers. He had shot twenty-three people and raped fifteen women.

Cedric Maupa Maake.

A Pedi, thirty-two years of age. Handyman, suburban gardener. Serial killer.

As one journalist from *Beeld* described him during the trial, Maake was a small, thin, fresh-faced young guy, someone you wouldn't hesitate to employ if he came knocking on your door on a Saturday morning.

On the way back to Brixton after he had been arrested, Piet watched Maake in the rear-view mirror. He saw his lips turn white.

"Do you feel all right?" Piet asked. Silence.

After an arrest Piet always watches the suspect, taking note of the way the suspect speaks to him, looks at him, or doesn't look at him. Piet is able to detect the slightest sign of nervousness – how the suspect keeps swallowing, for example. "I see the person. I immediately know if the person I've caught is the right one."

Cedric Maake's white lips gave him away.

At Brixton, Maake asked to see his wife. "I'll arrange it," Piet said. Mmm, his weak spot, Piet thought. But his face showed nothing.

In the meantime, Piet knew very well that he could detain Maake for only forty-eight hours – the window period during which he would have to collect enough evidence to charge him.

First he arranged for a blood sample so that it could be compared to the DNA profile the police already had of the murderer. The technicians at the forensic lab in Pretoria worked right through Christmas so that they could have the results ready before the deadline was up.

Only hours before the cut-off time, Captain Luhein Frazenburg of the forensic division phoned with the news: the DNA matched. It was the same man.

"Suddenly Christmas had come for me too!" Piet says.

But Piet's client was in no party mood. Neither were the two policemen who had to guard him at Brixton. Piet grins. "The shit was literally flying, and they had to duck to avoid it! Maake was throwing his own faeces at them, screaming like a stuck pig."

As with Mazingane, Piet had to rush to Brixton in the middle of the night to calm the man down.

When he arrived at Maake's filthy cell, Piet asked casually. "Can I get you a cooldrink? You might as well know you're not getting out of here. You can do what you like but it would be better not to upset the people around here."

Piet then offered him a cigarette. No, Maake shouted, he doesn't smoke. Nevertheless he took the cigarette and put it behind his ear before breaking it into pieces. Piet stood there, watching, impassive.

"I spent two, three hours with him. He swore at me and carried on, repeating over and over that he had no idea what I was talking about.

"Later I said: I've been so kind to you. I fetched your wife, and I'll bring her again if you want me to. And your mother …"

Maake really cared for his mother. Piet had learned that earlier from Maake's wife. He used this information to calm Maake down.

If you talk to Piet's colleagues, they'll all mention Piet's endless patience with suspects. Other investigating officers often become irritated, but not Piet. He seldom gets angry, but when it does happen, it's highly effective. He uses anger only to get results. Piet Byleveld is one of those rare people who are in full control of their emotions.

The next day, DNA results in hand, Piet confronted Maake in his office.

"Cedric, I know it's you who killed all those people at Wemmer Pan, raped the women and did all those things.

"He watched me in silence for about a minute. The next moment he said, almost proudly, 'Yes, I did it. It was me.'

"He admitted it. Right there in my office." Piet smiles, savouring the moment once more.

"The thing is, serial killers won't stop until they are caught. Actually, they want to get caught. And it's my job to catch them."

Piet arranged for Maake to point out the murder scenes in the company of an independent officer and an interpreter. "It's important to do it immediately, before the suspect gets cold feet," says Piet.

Maake took them to more than forty sites, including the one where he had shot "the white man" (Gerhard Lavoo) beside Wemmer Pan for his bicycle.

The clothing and shoes he had taken from his victims were stored with his mother in Giyane, near Tzaneen in the former Northern Province, he told Piet.

Mazingane had left the shoes of the women he raped neatly next to their bodies.

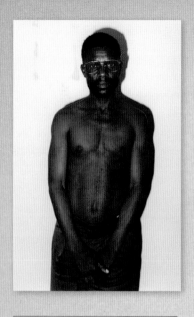

Cedric Maake after his arrest.

A handbag found at a murder scene.

One of Maake's victims found lying in a foetal position.

Maake often removed his victims' shoes.

Maake points out a scene to Piet.

Maake generally only took one shoe from the male victim.

"Do all serial killers leave messages and clues for their investigators, as profilers and detective series like csi would have us believe?" I ask.

"With respect, that's nonsense," Piet says brusquely, keen to put paid to the idea. "In not one of my cases did that happen. It's a theory that is encouraged for the purpose of sensationalism."

Piet sniffs at such gimmicks. "I never work with a profiler. I make sure of the true facts, as they appear in front of me, ma'am. Facts. They give more than enough information." In spite of the stuffy Piet-speak, his eyes are twinkling mischievously.

He takes a piece of biltong from his friend's snack tray and lowers it furtively to Seuntjie, who is lying at his feet under the table. Meisie, the other fox terrier, lives with Esmie.

Dogs, it appears, also get divorced.

On 29 December 1997, Piet and his team set off with Maake for Giyane.

It was another typical soft-soap trip of Piet's, with chats about sport, offers of a radio in his cell, and a copy of the *Sowetan* lying on the seat for the suspect to read in the car.

When they finally arrived at their destination, they found in Malekgolo Maake's township house a pile of clothes and shoes. Here was her son's macabre loot.

Malekgolo was clearly devastated when she saw her son, Cedric, in police custody. Piet left them alone for a while.

Malekgolo had been the first wife of Cedric Maake's father. He'd got married again, and after that, Cedric and his mother had played second fiddle. The cattle had been divided up and the second marriage had left Cedric's mother poorer.

"It broke Cedric," says Piet. "He told me that he hated his father with a passion."

On their way back that evening, Piet and Maake's conversation in the car was forthright and easy.

Then, out of the blue, Maake offered to show Piet where he had hidden the pistol.

It was late, about half past ten, when they stopped in the Wemmer Pan area. It was also pitch-dark and it had begun to rain. Maake led the way, with Piet and the two sergeants in tow. They felt their way past a flattened mine dump, until they were behind a tree.

"You won't believe it but even in that darkness he went straight to the spot. Suddenly he bent down. Luckily I was on guard. Bloody hell! He was going to surprise me, grab the pistol and shoot me."

Piet ignored Maake all the way back to Brixton. No more chit-chat. In the boot, safe in a plastic bag, was Exhibit 1: the pistol.

"When the report came back from ballistics, I knew there was no way he was going to get out of it. Victory."

By this time Piet had already "got inside Maake's head" and found out everything he could about him. Now he knew even the smallest details about the killer and how he operated, yet very little was known about Maake's childhood. He came from Thohoyandou in Limpopo Province. He went to school until standard seven before coming to Gauteng, where he did painting and gardening jobs. His employers trusted him implicitly.

"One of his brothers is a police sergeant. Interesting, isn't it? The same home, the same circumstances. But that very brother later offered me a R500 bribe to help Cedric."

Maake had met his wife, Sophie, in Giyane. When he discovered that she'd had affairs with other men, the fat was in the fire. He discovered that she'd had sex with them on a nearby koppie. That was why he later chased his victims up mine dumps before raping and killing them, Maake told Piet.

While he was in detention, Maake would intimidate the policemen at the Brixton charge office. He unnerved them to such an extent that they refused to speak to him and even asked the station commander to send him straight to prison.

The homeowners at 57 Forest Street, La Rochelle, where Maake and Sophie had been living in the garage, were frightened out of their wits when they learned that the "nice Cedric" they knew was actually the Wemmer Pan serial killer.

He had been a perfect, quiet tenant. In his room, detectives found more 9mm cartridges.

They found Sophie there too. The poor woman didn't have an inkling.

Piet laughs, a belly laugh. Yep. Serial killers look like … anybody. Your gardener. Your taxi driver. Your husband. They conceal their underlying aggression very well; they usually work alone; they take no one into their confidence; they have memories like elephants and are extremely cunning.

Trying to catch one, Piet says, is like playing chess against a grandmaster. And catching one … He draws long and deeply on his cigarette.

And then, with Maake a new member of Piet's exclusive group of prisoners, the Piet Specials, one of the biggest breakthroughs in Piet Byleveld's career was lurking murderously around the next corner.

JEPPE'S HAMMER MURDERER

"Tailor," says the sign in the window of the tiny shop in Jeppe, an old, rundown area in the south-east of Johannesburg. A man glances furtively up and down the street before pushing open the door. A bell clangs and an elderly Indian man looks up from his sewing machine.

It smells of spices and furniture polish and age. Rolls of dusty fabric lie piled up in shelves behind him.

The man hands over a shirt for mending. Haggles about the price. The tailor nods, makes out an order form, pins it to the shirt and turns around to place it on the shelf behind him.

The customer jumps forward, pulls out a four-pound hammer and hits the tailor on the head, just behind the right ear. He sinks to the floor without making a sound.

The man helps himself to the few rands in the old cash register, takes his shirt and a pair of trousers from a hanger behind the counter and calmly walks to the door. He closes it behind him, crosses the street and is gone.

The old man in the shop is dead, his head lying in a pool of blood on the wooden floor.

"It was 1997, around November … " Piet Byleveld recalls. "In the Jeppe area Indian tailors were being murdered one after another, all with a hammer blow behind the head."

Heads together, we huddle over his scrapbooks. It's late afternoon, the biltong is finished, the Amstels have been cracked, the voice is somewhat hoarse after hours of reminiscing about his most difficult client: Cedric Maupa Maake.

"So, I was quite busy. On weekends it was the Wemmer Pan killings, on weekdays the Jeppe tailors and in between the Nasrec and Kranskop murders."

Piet gets up from the mahogany-brown leather sofa and paces up and down in the living room of his townhouse.

He can't sit still – has never been able to, in fact.

At Brixton, he remembers, 1997 went by in a flurry of work.

"In those days I had no personal life. I just worked. And managed to spend as little time as possible at home.

"I did the housekeeping, tended my little garden. Over the years the household had always been my responsibility. I bought the groceries because I disliked getting home late at night only to discover that there was no milk or bread."

In the middle of a High Court trial in which he was giving evidence, Esmie phoned one day to say that she was seriously ill. He had to come at once. The session was adjourned there and then to give Piet a chance to go home.

"When I arrived, she said she had a headache and wanted painkillers. It happened regularly that she'd phone while I was at work because she urgently needed something. She expected me to drop everything to go and buy it for her.

"She regularly accused me of having affairs with senior female colleagues and of fathering illegitimate children. And that wasn't all: I was also accused of having a homosexual relationship with a high-ranking official of the High Court."

He speaks of how he spent his evenings in pubs so that he wouldn't have to go home. When he finally did go home, he used to sit in his car, afraid of the confrontation that would be waiting inside. Later, after the customary shouting match, he would get back into his car and simply drive, once all the way to Bela Bela.

"The marriage was a mistake. A mistake." His voice is strained.

"And Elize Smit?" I enquire cautiously.

All I get is a slight smile. "No," he says, "let's carry on. Let's talk about the hammer murders in Jeppe."

The Indian tailors in Jeppe usually worked alone in their small shops. They were all soft targets, like seventy-four-year-old Hariji Vandaya. They ran small businesses, with names such as Boston Tailors, Jay's Wholesalers, Levios Shoe Repairs, Modern Tailors, Korolia Stores, KB Patel Tailors.

There were numerous attacks. In a matter of weeks, Piet investigated twenty-seven cases of murder and attempted murder resulting from hammer assaults. Some of the survivors suffered severe brain damage. They would never sit at their sewing machines again.

The traders of Jeppe were upset. Terrified. The tailors among them were being decimated and no one had been brought to book. Some of the shops had closed their doors.

Piet and his team began with intensive enquiries – they literally walked the streets, asking the residents: have you seen any suspicious-looking characters hanging around?

In the meantime, the hammer murderer was casting his net ever wider. His next victim was a café owner. Antonio Afonso of the Hill Extension Gardens Café was robbed and seriously injured.

Finally, an unexpected breakthrough came. It was one of the many loose ends in Piet's Wemmer Pan investigation that he was trying to tie up.

Piet Byleveld hates loose ends.

Cedric Maake was barely in custody when Piet asked him what he had done with Gerhard Lavoo's bicycle. It's at a pawn shop, Maake replied.

"On 12 January 1998, Cedric took me to Billy's Pawn Shop in La Rochelle in the south of Johannesburg. He had sold the bicycle there for R120. On the receipt he had used the alias Patrick Mokwena."

Patrick Mokwena … gears were suddenly clicking in Piet's brain.

"I stared at the receipt and realised it was the same name the hammer murderer had used on a lay-by receipt in an Indian shop. Bloody hell … the same man! At Wemmer Pan he shot them and in Jeppe he hit them with a hammer."

The detectives that had been at the crime scene in the Indian shop before Piet became involved, had already searched the place for clues. But they had missed the lay-by receipt. As always, Piet later went there himself, simply because Piet was Piet. Beyond thorough, he went through the shop with a fine-tooth comb, looking for traces, any clues that the others might have missed. He scrutinised the lay-by slips, making a mental note of the name on the last one.

He smiles, and I see a look of gratification on his face. "Standing in Billy's Pawn Shop with the bicycle receipt in my hand, the penny dropped when I read the name on it … bingo. For months I thought I was investigating two serial killers. Then the Wemmer Pan murderer and the hammer murderer turned out to be one and the same person."

"And," he smiles cynically, "I even got the bicycle back."

The Indian man in whose store they had found the receipt died of his injuries shortly after the trial, but a signature written in his shop had led to the breakthrough that brought a measure of closure to the loved ones of all the murdered tailors – and the community of Jeppe.

Of course, Maake had neglected to mention either hammers or tailors to Piet.

Back at Brixton, Piet had Maake brought to him and once again faced the killer across the government desk in office 105. Piet looked at Maake; Maake looked at Piet.

"Cedric, you operated in Jeppe too, didn't you?"

Yes, Maake nodded.

"What was your business with the tailors?"

Silence. Maake looked at Piet for a long time. Then he answered reluctantly, "Sometimes I took my clothes to be mended, because they had been torn and so on."

Why?

"Because the women would fight while I was raping them."

Silence again.

And then finally Cedric talked. In fact, he bawled out his murders, one after the other. Not because there was a relationship of trust between him and Piet – there never really was. He wasn't confessing, he was boasting. It was the megalomania of a sadist.

He pointed out murder scenes in the Jeppe area – murders Piet had not even been aware of. Maake was so arrogant that he had killed someone with a hammer barely a block from the Brixton charge office.

Piet asked: "Why tailors, Cedric?"

He looked up, first at the ceiling, then at Piet, as if it should have been obvious. See, once he had taken his shirt in and he wasn't satisfied with the mending. That was when he had begun to kill them.

No one fucked with Cedric's shirts.

While Maake was busy with his bizarre list of revelations, yet another group of victims came to light.

His victims had not only been single women, couples and tailors, but also elderly white men who had employed him to do odd jobs.

Maake pointed out murder scenes at several private residences. He would ask for work, then wait in the garden or garage for an opportunity to kill the old man with a blunt object.

He began to kill elderly white men because one apparently didn't pay him enough once.

He murdered Willem Johannes Petrus van Tonder on 28 November 1996 in Frankfort Street, South Hills. Van Tonder's son burst into tears during the trial, and the court had to be adjourned for an hour, *Beeld* newspaper reported.

The photos in the docket show Van Tonder's body lying on the carpet next to the wardrobe, his bloody head behind the bedside table, hidden under a lace curtain. On a crocheted cloth on the bedside table lies a publication of the Pentecostal Church. The house is neat as a pin. There's fruit in a bowl on the kitchen table. Sad, silent evidence of the orderly life of a religious man.

Piet Byleveld's dark eyes have seen hundreds, thousands of similar scenes of brutal cruelty. The props are just arranged differently.

"What has it done to you?" I ask.

The question hangs between us. A weary expression slides over his face.

"How do I feel? You never get used to that kind of violence. Never. But if you do this work, you don't think too deeply about the fate of the victims. You focus on the investigation. Focus On The Investigation. I stay in the moment. The victim is dead, and now I have a job to do. That's what it's about. I keep my eye on the ball."

Not everyone can manage to do it, though.

One of Piet's administrative assistants couldn't maintain that distance. It broke her psychologically.

"She had to deal with the forensic photographs, that kind of thing. She cracked, and had to leave. It all depends on your person-ality. Either you're wired for this game, or you're not."

He speaks in a measured tone.

"Let me tell you, many of my colleagues will never be able to do what I do. Serial killings aren't everyone's cup of tea. Especially when children are involved."

Cedric Maake in front of a tailor's shop.

Maake pointing out the scene of a crime.

Maake in cuffs.

Murder weapons.

Piet hesitates. Decides to ask the question anyway. "Do you think I'm a bit crazy?"

His dark eyes look for an answer. My chest tightens. It must be the cigarette smoke.

Cedric Maake's hunting ground was one of the first to be charted with modern profiling methods. It was the first serial-killing trial in South Africa during which the Geographic Information System (GIS), which makes use of cartography, statistic analyses and database technology, was used.

What made the Maake case especially interesting was that the police initially compiled two separate profiles because the Wemmer Pan and hammer murders had completely divergent patterns.

Dr Kim Rossmo, the Canadian expert on serial killings, had a particular interest in the case. Rossmo was especially fascinated by Maake, who, with more than five different modi operandi, had rewritten the textbook on serial killers along with Mazingane and Mfeka – all of them eventually deviating from their initial target area and victim types. "But Cedric Maake was the most perfect serial killer of them all," says Piet.

Rossmo, a pioneer in the field of criminal profiling, had developed a mathematical model, according to which the most likely dwelling place of a serial killer could be plotted.

With Rossmo's help, a large aerial photograph of the area where Maake attacked was used during the trial. Red dots marked the places where he had killed and raped.

GIS is used as an aid to find serial killers, but in this instance Rossmo used it as a case study and an experiment. It showed that the majority of Maake's murders were committed within 500 metres of his two places of residence, his place of work and his brother and girlfriend's homes. The same pattern had been found with Mazingane. He too had killed within 500 metres of his living quarters.

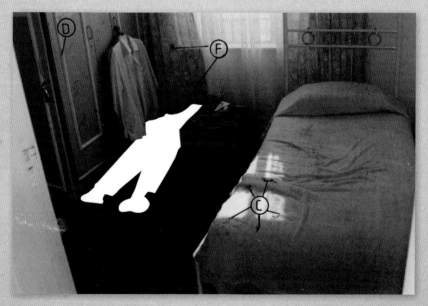

The murder scene of Willem Johannes Petrus van Tonder.

Smoke break. Piet is stretching his legs in his garden. The fish pond, constructed of fake rocks, is newly cemented in. It has been relocated from Weltevreden Park. A fish is swimming round and round. The flowerbeds are full of new seedlings Piet has selected with care – one of these days the garden will be an oasis of colour, just like his previous one.

"Have I told you," he makes small talk, "about the time Piet Byleveld, the detective, you know, was liberated of his cellphone at the traffic light at the Beyers Naude off-ramp?

"I heard a crash to my right. At first I thought someone was shooting at me. At the time there was a price of half a million rand on my head, arranged from inside prison by a drug syndicate. When the window was smashed, I reacted so fast that I struck the robber in the face with my elbow as he was grabbing my cellphone."

Piet gave chase, of course. But his age and the cigarettes counted against him. The thief got away with the cellphone of an ace detective.

If the smash-and-grab thief had known exactly whom he had made a fool of he would undoubtedly still be boasting about it to this day on the grass verges beside the highway.

The big preparation for the trial began. There were more than 300 witnesses, and Piet and his team consulted with each of them. It took eight months.

The dockets of the Wemmer Pan and hammer murders were combined. The inventory, *All murders committed by Cedric Maake*, filled three pages, typed in single spacing, with names, names, names …

During consultation with Maake, even more murders emerged. Their locations had not been pointed out by the killer.

"He didn't give a damn who he killed," says Piet.

Meanwhile, Maake had become quite familiar and started calling him Piet. The detective, however, dealt with Maake in his usual unemotional way; just being "a smooth operator", as he calls it.

The trial lasted 358 days. The prosecutor was Advocate Gerrit Roberts, Deputy Director of Public Prosecution at the Witwatersrand, aided by Advocate Yolinda du Plessis.

Wemmer Pan was the first big case during which Advocate Gerrit Roberts (sc) and Piet ("a policeman of the old school", as Roberts calls him) co-operated. A close relationship has since developed between them, so much so that he regards Piet as a friend and not just another policeman, Roberts says.

"Piet is a decent man," he continues, sharing the story about the day when Piet was too polite to smoke in front of Roberts's wife. "Piet was smoking in my office at the High Court when my wife arrived unexpectedly. He immediately hid the cigarette in his closed hand and stubbed it out in the pocket of his suit jacket!"

Piet leaves no stone unturned once he smells blood, Roberts continues. "He doesn't accept anything at face value, and leaves nothing to chance. Everything is painstakingly investigated and every last detail exposed."

Piet Byleveld and Gerrit Roberts sent Maake to jail for the rest of his life.

On 26 April 1999, Piet sat behind piles of court files in Court 2F in the Johannesburg High Court and watched Cedric Maake climb the steps from the court cells to the dock.

His client was facing an astonishing 134 charges.

Although some of the victims who survived the hammer attacks had sustained serious brain damage, Roberts and his team put those witnesses on the stand. All they were required to say was the name of their business and where they had incurred their injury: behind the left or right ear. This was only to prove that a crime had been committed.

When the trial began, the easy camaraderie between Piet and Maake completely evaporated, and Piet even got death threats from the family.

In the dock, where Maake sat for eleven months, mostly with his head resting on his knees, he would come to life whenever he saw Piet and curse him in the foulest language imaginable. Every time his mother's name was mentioned Maake became emotional as well. On one occasion he went berserk and it took six hefty policemen to restrain him.

The victims' relatives found it hard to endure the evidence that detailed Maake's atrocious deeds. Mariëtte de Caires wept uncontrollably. The skull of her husband, Jose, had been crushed with a hammer in his garage. Lelanie van Wyk's mother, Klaressa, testified that she had been so traumatised by her daughter's death that she had suffered a light stroke. She had only been able to identify Lelanie by the Minnie Mouse tattoo on her shoulder. Martin Stander's mother, Alberta, and Hazel Pietersen, the mother of Pieter John du Plessis, who was shot dead with his girlfriend during the same killing spree, both told the court, in tears, about their horror and grief, and how they could not come to terms with the deaths of their sons.

"Charlotte Ndlovu, one of the victims who had survived, was present in court. Her friend, Jerry Naidoo, had been shot dead," Piet remembers. "She couldn't testify, but she told me the case was killing her, that it affected her every single day."

Dr Patricia Klepp, senior state pathologist, testified that never before in her long career had she seen such relentless assaults as those that had been made on the tailors.

In his evidence for mitigation, Dr Saths Cooper, a clinical psychologist, gave an interesting perspective on the psyche of this killer. Maake, he said, could not control his anger under specific circumstances.

Jose de Caires was found in his garage.

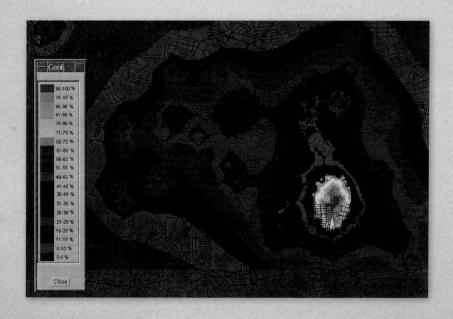

The Geographic Information System indicating the concentration of murders at Wemmer Pan.

"His anger will abate only after he has killed someone," Cooper said. "He cannot control himself before the anger has been spent. He's not a psychopath, though he shows signs of being one."

Maake drew Cooper a sketch, little more than a stick figure that a grade-one learner would be able to improve on. According to Cooper, the sketch showed Maake's obsession with shoes and soccer, and was typical of his distorted view of life.

Maake never told anyone why he had committed his savage deeds. Piet had spent many days interrogating him, but Maake never really took Piet into his confidence. His answers shed no light on why he did what he did, and his motives remain a mystery, as experts testified during the trial.

No, Piet says, there's no mystery. It was all about power. Maake wanted to be in control. And he kept killing because subconsciously he wanted to be caught. That was why he didn't conceal the bodies.

The rest is speculation, Piet says. Perhaps it was his wife's affairs that made him rape women, and the men – whom he referred to as dogs – were murdered to take revenge on his wife's lovers. We'll never know why he took their shoes.

What Piet does know is that in his entire career he had never before come across anyone with such innate cruelty.

"He was completely without feeling. He would look you in the eye and there would be no trace of emotion. Ever. He had outbursts, sure, but he never succumbed to emotion."

Piet narrows his eyes. "Cedric, I'm telling you, was the worst of the worst. It was unquestionably the most complex case of my career."

The judgment took four and a half days. On 13 March 2000, when Judge Geraldine Borcherds sentenced Maake, he was reclining in the dock with his hands cradling his head. He was asleep.

Piet sat quietly among the next of kin, his "duty to the

community" over, as he later formally worded it to the media on the steps in front of the court building.

Cedric Maupa Maake was handed twenty-seven life sentences and an additional 1 159 years and three months' imprisonment for twenty-seven murders, twenty-six attempted rapes, fourteen rapes, forty-one robberies and eleven counts of attempted robbery.

A total of 2 214 years in prison. And when that is over, another three months …

After his sentence had been handed down, Maake left the court-room, smiling. He was on his way to C-Max, the maximum security prison in Pretoria.

Today he sits there in solitary confinement. All on his own, this human volcano. Confined. Caged. Forever.

BODIES IN THE WATER

"What are you doing?" asks the young man, startled, when his two friends suddenly overpower him, tie him up and bundle him into the car.

They stop at Bruma Lake. It's the dead of night. The man struggles as they lift him out of the car and carry him to the water's edge. The water is deep and black. He is terrified. He knows what is coming.

The two swing the body wide over the water and let go. The splash breaks the silence of the night. They look around to see whether anyone has seen them, then casually walk back to the car, get in and drive away.

In the dark waters of the lake the bricks that have been tied to the man drag his body slowly to the bottom. He struggles in vain. His lungs are burning.

What does he think of just before he loses consciousness? The village where he grew up, thousands of kilometres away in the African savannah? His father's face, his mother's gentle smile? Or is there only panic, the knowledge that his family will be waiting for him in vain ...

Then everything goes dark one last time.

B ruma Lake. "This is how you turn a fuck-up into a feature," Piet Byleveld says, and he tells me that he still smiles about that every time he drives past this man-made lake in the east of Johannesburg.

The once stinking sewage catchment area was given a serious face-lift some years ago and changed into a waterfront development with restaurants, shops and offices on its banks. At the time it was one of the first of its kind in the country and initially it was a huge success. A flea market developed on its banks and grew into the largest in South Africa, with more than 600 vendors – with drug trafficking, hijacking and black marketeering as shady side-effects.

Over the years, however, the lake gradually silted up so that by 2010 there was only about four centimetres of water sitting on a layer of sludge and sewage almost two metres deep. Only after numerous businesses had closed their doors and a chorus of protest had gone up from the residents in the area, did the Johannesburg municipality start to think of ways to rehabilitate the lake.

For years the lake had been used as a clandestine dumping site. Anything from garden refuse and false teeth to old washing machines found its way to the lake's filthy water. From sewage back to sewage, one might say.

Then, in 2000, a new ingredient was added to the soupy mix. Bodies.

Early in January 2001, when a third bloated body floated to the surface in the hot summer sun, Commissioner Perimal Naidoo had had enough. Why were his men not making progress? Two restaurants and a hair salon had closed since the first body surfaced on the turbid water nine months earlier. Imagine this: you're sitting in an open-air restaurant, enjoying your steak, when all of a sudden a body floats by.

Everything pointed to another serial killer on the loose.

The cry went up: get the serial killer boffin. Naidoo phoned Piet

Byleveld. Take over the case, and solve it – and quickly. That was Piet's brief.

Superintendent Petrus Erasmus Johannes van Staden Byleveld is the name that is laboriously written on the cover of his Bruma Lake statement.

"Come to attention when you say those names," he teases me.

Today he is wearing new khaki trousers his girlfriend chose for him, and a fashionable checked shirt. His 1970s slip-on sandals have been replaced by designer sneakers in a seventies retro style. Truly.

He looks like a different man. Not so cop-like anymore. He even drinks red wine nowadays. Always Four Cousins. He rattles off the name: Forcousins.

Love has bowled the Byl over. Truly.

On the lawn a "chicken-in-beer" perches in the Weber, sizzling. Seuntjie sniffs around the flowerbeds. The doves peck at the crumbs Piet has thrown out.

Girlfriend Elize is doing some serious shopping. Christmas is just around the corner. Her shopping list looks like a store inventory, Piet jokes.

Last night the two of them sat outside on the stoep, chatting. The next thing they knew, it was past two in the morning. They never run out of things to say, Piet says, almost surprised, as if he can hardly believe it himself, this happiness that has crept up on him so unexpectedly.

For the first time in decades Piet Byleveld is happy. Truly happy.

When the Bruma case landed in his lap Piet Byl had not lost a case in his whole career. His reputation as a super-sleuth was firmly established. His name was engraved on the Suiker Britz floating trophy. He was one of the "Ysters" (Irons) – Commissioner Britz's name for the crème de la crème of his specialist detectives – "old-school" alumni who would leave no stone unturned to solve a case. "24/7 detectives", Advocate Gerrit Roberts calls them.

Among these detectives the competition has always been as thick as the smoke-filled air in their offices. Whereas his colleagues might have been somewhat indifferent to him in earlier days, some of them now started maintaining a distance. Envy might have played a role, Piet reckons.

"At the Brixton reunion braais the conversation would peter out when I joined them at the fire. Some of them weren't exactly rude, but neither were they friendly. Perhaps I got too much attention from the media."

Piet was therefore not altogether surprised when he ran into a stubborn investigator who refused to hand over the Bruma case dockets to him. Eventually, and with great difficulty, he managed to get hold of three dockets.

"The victims were black men, all clad in shorts. Their feet were tied together; some had rocks tied to the ropes to drag the body down. It was clearly murder. Serial killings."

The question on everyone's lips was: how many bodies are still at the bottom of the lake? Piet decided the lake had to be drained. Advocate Gerrit Roberts agreed. "Empty the lake," he told Piet.

It was a contentious decision. An empty, stinking lake could negatively affect the entire environment as well as cause the already struggling business centre on the banks to lose even more tenants. But Piet stuck to his guns.

It took two days for all the water to be drained. The high-ranking officials at Anglo American, who owned the complex, were furious. The municipality was equally irate. The entire area stank to high heaven and Piet's professional credibility was at stake. "The only ones who weren't angry were the birds. They had a ball among the dead fish," Piet remarks.

He laughs when he remembers the advocate who contacted him,

asking him to look for his fiancée's engagement ring at the bottom of the lake, now that it was empty. In a moment of dramatic rage following an argument between them, she had tossed the ring into the lake.

Rubber-booted policemen and dogs were sent into the filthy mire to look for bodies. There were furniture, supermarket trolleys, clothes, bottles and beer cans. And piles of dead fish.

But not a single body. And no ring.

Piet laughs again. He knows all about discarded engagement rings. "Esmie threw away two during temper tantrums. The first time I searched for the ring, but I couldn't find it. Later I felt sorry for her and bought her a new one. But when, after yet another argument, she threw that one away too, I didn't even bother to look." His two rings are still just as missing as the advocate's one.

It still peeves Piet that the lake wasn't cleaned before it was refilled. "They just filled it with water, right over all that mud and slush and rubbish. It bothered me terribly."

More businesses at Bruma closed after the water had been drained. Piet's fault, everyone said. Some even predicted that the entire development would shut down.

Then Advocate André de Vries, Director of Public Prosecution of the Witwatersrand, marched into Piet's office, and told him he wanted an arrest before the end of April.

"That was a mere three months away," Piet sighs, shaking his head.

At the Johannesburg High Court, De Vries had a special office set up as a permanent working space for Piet. The two men had known each other for years, and the Saturday afternoon beer they enjoyed at a local pub had become a tradition for them.

That office was a concession that no other detective had ever been given. The fact that Piet had almost full-time involvement with various court cases that were often simultaneously underway clinched the "reward". That, and his reputation as a detective who never dropped the ball during a trial.

The walls of his office at the court were lined with photos of bodies, maps, notes – it was the ops room of a serial-killer specialist.

On a table to one side stood the electric oxygen apparatus he used every morning. It was always close at hand, as was his inhaler. His asthma gave him hell, growing worse as his stress levels increased. "The closer to a trial, the more my chest would tighten."

Piet always stressed terribly about the witnesses. Were they going to turn up? Were they going to be credible? Would they stick to their statements? What if they let him down?

The inhaler worked only up to a point, however, and Advocate André Smith was often the one who had to rush Piet to hospital when he started to turn blue in court.

"It's a terrible feeling when you can't breathe. You can't move, you can't think, you panic; it's as if you're frozen," Piet explains.

One day it was so bad, the paramedics found Piet clinging desperately to the security gate at the front door of his townhouse in Weltevreden Park, sweating and blue in the face.

They had arrived just in time. A few minutes later and Piet would have died.

On 8 February 2001, Piet received a call from the Germiston police station.

Two men had been arrested at Rhodes Park in Kensington, not far from Bruma, for the illegal possession of two firearms. They were Themba Nkosi (22) and Simon Majola (35), both from Hillbrow.

Something about the profiles of the two aroused Piet's suspicion. "Keep the suspects there," he said. "I'm on my way."

"When I arrived, the two men were pretty cocky. The younger one, Nkosi, was dressed according to the latest fashion. He seemed to find his arrest a big joke. Majola was much quieter though; I think he realised he was in serious trouble. 'I'm taking you through to Brixton,' I told them. 'And if I were you I would use the time to think.'"

The two knew very well who Piet Byleveld was. And what they were supposed to think about.

They were taken to Brixton in separate vehicles. Even before they arrived, Piet noticed that the muscular Nkosi's lips had begun to tremble. The trusted formula was working: the Byleveld plus Brixton fear equation.

Piet made them sit in separate offices. First Nkosi cried, then he talked. And he didn't talk only about the three murders at Bruma, but also about incidents in Rhodes Park, where they had robbed people, about the murder of a Baptist pastor on 15 May 2000, and about a housebreaking, during the course of which they had killed their friend.

The two later pointed out the crime scenes, as well as others in Rhodes Park, of which Piet hadn't been aware.

It turned out to be a ridiculously easy case to crack, but, as Piet knew only too well, no investigation is over before the judge has delivered his verdict. Things can still go wrong in court. The two could easily have been acquitted; there were no eyewitnesses, only the confessions they had made. "Remember, they were arrested for the illegal possession of a firearm, and not on any other charges."

Simon Majola and Themba Nkosi had met each other while partying in Hillbrow, had become friends and then later upgraded the friendship to a partnership in crime.

Between 29 April 2000 and 7 February 2001 the two conducted a reign of terror, not only at Bruma but also at three parks in the east of Johannesburg: Rhodes Park, Bezuidenhout Park and Observatory Rift Park. They would ambush unsuspecting lovers at party and picnic spots in the late afternoon and evening.

Their modus operandi was simple. They would overpower their

victims with a firearm or knife and demand: give us your car, cellphones, bank cards, clothes, money and jewellery, or we'll throw you into the lake alive. Once they even stole a set of building plans.

Many incidents were never reported. Some of the couples they had targeted were gay and reluctant to come forward.

Whenever one of their friends discovered what they were up to and they felt that there was a possibility that he might speak out, Nkosi and Majola would unceremoniously tie bricks or rocks to his feet and drown him in Bruma Lake.

Two of the three bodies that the police found in Bruma Lake were so badly decomposed that they were never identified. They were recorded as "adult male", presumably from somewhere in Africa. Four bodies were also found in the Rhodes Park area. Identikits were compiled and published in the media, but there was no response from the public as to who the victims might be. The only evidence the police had was a pair of red checked boxer shorts and a green windbreaker jacket that had been found on the bodies of two of the unidentified victims. The last body, found on 5 January, still had a gold ring on his right hand which the murderers had not even bothered to remove. *The Star* reported that the man was dressed in a *Daily Express* T-shirt with a Rugby World Cup picture of Nelson Mandela and Francois Pienaar printed on the front.

Piet smiles at me. "The faces of celebrities show up in the weirdest places, don't they? Imagine the image of Madiba and Francois on a T-shirt on a body at the bottom of a muddy lake ..."

Nkosi turned out to be a real cowboy, Piet continues. He would graciously give his victims a choice: "How do you want to die? Shall I shoot you? Or must we drown you? Which do you choose?"

One victim who had escaped with his life, Eddie Mawela, later testified about the gentleman robber who had taken his car and clothes at Bezuidenhout Park and then gallantly apologised to his

Simon Majola and Themba Nkosi in court.

Aerial photos of Bruma Lake shown during the trial.

girlfriend because he had touched her breasts while searching her. *Beeld* reported that when it had begun to rain, Nkosi had felt suddenly sorry for Mawela and allowed him to put his trousers back on.

As gallant as the flamboyant Nkosi could sometimes be, his behaviour on other occasions could be sadistically cruel. He regularly boasted to his girlfriend, Jabulile Lushaba, that he was the notorious serial killer about whom the newspapers were reporting, and would hold forth about how he and Majola controlled the area. He assaulted her appallingly and frequently threatened to drown her as well.

Later she proved to be a good witness in court and her vengeance was sweet: Nkosi was found guilty of assaulting her with the intent to do grievous bodily harm.

The new millennium was only two weeks old when Claude Nolte of Alberton and his girlfriend, Simone Rousseau, drew into the parking area of Rhodes Park. Shortly afterwards the attackers pounced. Nolte kept a panga in his car. Panga in hand, he jumped out of the car to defend himself but the two attackers overpowered him and threatened to hack him to death with his own panga and to shoot him as well.

Desperately, Claude tried to save himself. Later, in court, he testified how he had desperately shouted at them: "No, I'm a Christian. God is watching you. He never forgets."

Then they shot him. The first shot just missed him but the second lodged in his left thigh. They took his girlfriend's cellphone and handbag and vanished with her into the dark, where they later set her free, unharmed. Claude, on the other hand, lay there, fearing he was going to bleed to death. Eventually he was found by the police, recovered completely and became an excellent witness in court.

But Claude Nolte was one of the lucky ones. The range of this murderous pair's exploits was mirrored by the grieved evidence of their victims' next of kin, and there were many of them.

Len Baird, whose son Errol lived with murder victim Clyde Allen

Thomas in Kensington, told Judge Labuschagne about the horror of finding his son's companion dead in the driveway of their home.

Luis Miguel Nunes told the judge how they had searched frantically for his uncle, Manuel Aries Baptista, before finding him in the Johannesburg Hospital. Manuel Baptista had remained in a coma for about a week and *The Star* reported how Luis testified that his uncle had had "bruises all over his body. There were marks on his neck, indicating signs of an attempt to strangle him. He died a week later." During the trial, Nkosi was calm and polite, but when his lies and jokes began to backfire, he lost his temper. "I'm not Jesus Christ to be held responsible for others' sins," he snarled at the prosecutor.

His mother, Ruth Tsheno, a simple, deeply religious woman, delivered an emotional plea on her son's behalf in mitigation of sentence. She could not believe that her eldest child was capable of such cruelty. He had always looked after his younger siblings so caringly when she had gone to church; she had trusted him with her life.

She hadn't known that Nkosi had a girlfriend and was shocked to learn he had assaulted the heavily pregnant Jabulile and kicked her in the stomach. The baby later died during birth.

While the poor woman was testifying, Nkosi laughed in his mother's face. At one point she looked him in the eye and murmured: "No, this is not my son."

Majola impressed Piet, however, especially when, at some point, the two men fired their legal representatives and Majola took over their defence himself.

"You won't believe how good he was under cross-examination. He countered State Advocate Herman Broodryk on every charge. He left nothing out. And the rap sheet was 200 pages long. In another life, another time, Majola would have made an excellent advocate."

One of the most bizarre moments of the trial was when Court 4B briefly turned into the meeting place of the "Serial Killer Club", Piet recalls.

When the case had to be postponed because Majola's legal representative had failed to turn up, it overlapped for a few minutes with the next case that was to be heard in Court 4B – that of the Nasrec serial killer, Lazarus Mazingane. For a while the three accused were in court simultaneously.

Majola, Nkosi and Mazingane embraced like old friends and struck up a conversation. Some of their relatives joined in and it almost turned into a party. The three even exchanged notes and telephone numbers.

Piet shakes his head. "It was a circus. Advocates Herman Broodryk, Gerrit Roberts and I stood there with our arms folded, watching them."

On 16 May 2002, after seventy-seven days in court and the testimonies of ninety-one witnesses, Judge Joop Labuschagne found Nkosi and Majola guilty on thirty-seven charges, including eight of murder and nineteen of robbery with aggravating circumstances.

Head lowered and cap in hand, Majola listened as he was handed eight life sentences plus another 422 years' imprisonment. Although he was married and had two children it was clear that he had chosen early in his life to be a criminal, and he had never shown any remorse for his crimes, Judge Labuschagne said.

Nkosi responded to his five life sentences plus another 253 years' imprisonment with a loud curse.

Court 4B was empty.

The two serial killers were behind bars. The judge had disappeared into his chambers. Piet stood outside, smoking.

Fifty minutes later, Lazarus Mazingane was escorted up the steps. Piet was back. Everyone was waiting for Judge Joop Labuschagne to re-enter and open the proceedings.

Bows were taken. Court 4B was back in session.

In the dock stood Nasrec's notorious rope knotter, small and grim in his prison uniform.

That evening, according to tradition, Herman Broodryk, Nicolette Bell, André Smith and Piet Byleveld walked up the steps of John Quenchers, their favourite hang-out in the centre of town. It was Piet's thank you to the state's legal team. They had scarcely sat down when waitress Dudu brought Piet his customary two Grandpas with his first ice-cold Amstel.

Then they partied.

"We celebrated our success. And yes, we also celebrated the fact that the Nasrec trial had begun at last. I thought at the time though: drink your beer, Piet, there's a difficult road ahead."

Some of Piet's colleagues criticised him after the trial, saying that all Piet had actually done was carry the dockets to court.

"I'm cheesed off about it, I can tell you that much! I worked hard for that guilty verdict."

Celebrity and the title of "super cop" certainly came unexpectedly for a man who had grown so accustomed to police dockets and years and years of hard, dour, thankless investigations.

After a while, there was the perception within the police force that Piet's new-found celeb status had gone straight to his head. This was exacerbated by the fact that he had never been "one of the boys", and had always been considered a bit of an outsider. Other members of the force labelled Piet "media hungry", and thought that he didn't really deserve the attention the media was giving him.

Celebrity, Piet had to learn, is like wearing a brand-new pair of shoes. They give you blisters before they are comfortably worn in. Awkward statements and quotes in the media made Piet sound conceited. This was oil on the fires of his critics. In addition, when fame started coming his way, Piet wasn't always discerning about where and with whom he socialised. He was overworked, there was nothing to go home to at night, and everybody seemed to be hanging on every word that came from his lips.

There were also those people who abused his name and others who tried to ride his wave of success. They exploited his loneliness and the disintegration of his marriage. Then there was Elize, suddenly bringing him a sense of stability at a time when he was losing his grip.

"Yes, my life was spiralling out of control. Everything happened too fast." Piet nods and fixes his eyes on his big birdcage which houses zebra finches, quails and a finch that, he claims, sounds just like a canary.

This is Piet's place of comfort now.

"Angel, did you remember the chicken?" Elize asks as she walks through the front door, her arms laden with Christmas gifts.

"Bloody hell!" Piet shouts before jumping up and rushing over to rescue the Sunday lunch.

As always, Elize is dressed to the nines, from her crisp, white blouse down to her high-heeled sandals.

Later, in the car, Piet can't stop talking about Elize. How she's always smiling, how she's curious about life, just like him.

The detective is in love.

Being with Elize is marvellous, he tells me. They like to go out, listen to music rather than watch TV – anything from Kurt Darren to Elvis. They like to dance, all alone in the townhouse. They decorated the Christmas tree together. "I can't even remember when last I had a Christmas tree. And now I'm hanging stars and angels and things!"

We laugh at the enthusiasm of a cynical old sleuth. It's the fever of a young man. It's still the Season of Firsts.

SIBILLE – A BOLT FROM THE BLUE

She comes driving up the tree-lined avenue of the suburb with its well-established houses. It's dark, just after seven-thirty on a hot, stuffy spring evening.

She parks on the pavement, under the lamp post, locks her silver Audi A3 and starts walking to the house for her weekly visit. She is tall and attractive in her T-shirt and skintight jeans.

No more than three metres from her car, the attacker grabs her, so roughly that there's an instant bruise on her arm.

The next moment a bolt from a crossbow pierces the thick ligaments between the first and second neck vertebrae. It enters under her right ear and lodges in her neck, protruding at the other end.

She is instantly paralysed. She falls down on the tarred surface, unconscious. She lies with her arms outstretched, the arrow embedded in her neck, the arrow's vanes a bright, macabre splash of colour in the street light.

Her attacker flees. Within seconds, it is all over.

Her handbag is still lying in the street. A wallet, car keys and pieces of a wooden puzzle lie scattered on the tarmac.

In hospital, fourteen hours later, the machines that are keeping her alive are switched off.

Sibille Zanner is dead.

Why do the neighbours' dogs keep barking? Harold Streibel wondered irritably. Perhaps that's Sibille now. He looked through the kitchen window to see whether she had arrived.

Harold and Birgit Streibel had been living at 18 Marble Crescent, Kloofendal, Roodepoort, for many years. Sibille was like a daughter to them, and the couple's cosy home provided her with a weekly escape from her work, children and home. They would enjoy a glass of red wine together and do craft projects, like the wooden puzzle Sibille was making for her children.

But tonight Sibille was late.

At that moment the doorbell rang. On his way to the door, Harold called out a greeting: "Hey, Sibille, you're late!"

But it was the neighbours. "Harold," they told him, "come and take a look outside, something's wrong."

"I stepped out into the driveway and there was Sibille, lying stretched out on the tar. I went closer and I saw something protruding from her neck. It looked like a pen. I noticed that her arm had a nasty bruise. It seemed almost unreal, as if someone had gently placed her there.

"The paramedics came, and then the police. They managed to restore her heartbeat, she was stabilised, lifted onto a stretcher and put into the ambulance. Then I phoned Sibille's husband, Frank."

We are in the Streibels' garden on a sunny morning in December 2009. Their daughter, Frauke, is also present. She and her family have come out from Germany for Christmas.

This morning, seven years after Sibille's death, the Streibels are reliving that "most awful day" with Piet and me.

25 September 2002. A Wednesday.

From time to time Piet joins us at the table, but he is restless. Every so often he's on the stoep, talking on his cellphone, smoking.

From our conversation with these people who loved her, a picture of Sibille gradually emerges.

The Streibels and the Zanners were old friends. Paul Zanner, a Johannesburg businessman, owned a factory that manufactured domestic cookware. Zanner's son, Frank, was probably meant to take over from him one day.

As time went by, however, the families drifted apart. They were moving in different circles. The Zanners had a yacht and there were regular trips abroad, Frauke tells us. According to Birgit, the glitzy lifestyle suited Frank, who was flamboyant and charming.

In the late 1980s, the Zanners invited Frauke to Europe on a skiing trip. Corina, Frank's sister, was Frauke's friend. Frank, who was living in Germany at the time, had just broken up with his girlfriend. One of his ex's friends, Sibille Breg, had caught his eye and so she was invited as well. That was where Frauke met Sibille. "She was about twenty-four or twenty-five and very pretty."

Sibille was all honey-coloured hair, honey-coloured legs. What was most attractive about her, however, was her vivacious personality. She and Frauke bonded instantly.

Sibille and Frank later came to spend Christmas with the Zanners in South Africa. "Everyone here took a liking to her because she was such fun, uncomplicated and unpretentious," Birgit Streibel says. "I told Frank she was good marriage material and, sure enough, on their way back to Germany, Frank proposed to Sibille."

They were married in Germany and Frank brought his bride back to South Africa, where he was appointed manager of his father's factory. The cream of the local German community attended their second wedding ceremony in Johannesburg.

Before buying their own home in Waterford Estate, Witkoppen, the newly-weds lived with Frank's parents. Sibille worked as a secretary for the German engineering firm Steinmüller, which supplied electric motors to mining companies, among others.

At one stage, she and Frauke drove to work together in the mornings. "We were young, the radio would be blaring and we would sing cheerful German songs. Sibille was the kind of friend that you could call at midnight and say, 'Let's go skinny-dipping in the neighbours' pool,' and she'd be game."

In 1993, after years of trying, Sibille fell pregnant. A baby girl, Bianca, was born. She was severely handicapped and lived for only three weeks. Birgit clearly remembers Sibille's composure and strength in hospital. When she saw how distressed Birgit was about Bianca, Sibille comforted her, telling her they should come to terms with the tragedy because nothing they could do would change the situation.

A few years later, Frank convinced Sibille to adopt twin boys. It took some persuasion because Sibille was uncertain whether she would be able to cope with two babies. But, Birgit says, she quickly became a loving, dedicated mother to the boys.

As is often the case, Sibille was of course the last one to hear that her husband was having an affair.

The Streibels had noticed that Frank was a bit distant. Birgit remembers that he seemed distracted and would sometimes doze off in company. Sibille realised that something was wrong with her marriage but couldn't figure out what, Birgit says.

In May 2002, six months before Sibille's death, Frank spilled the beans. He took Sibille out to dinner in a restaurant and confessed: for the past three years he'd been having an affair with a colleague, Susanna Hönigsperger. And that wasn't all. There was a child. A baby girl, born in August 2000.

"In other words, Frank knew his mistress was pregnant with his child when he persuaded Sibille to adopt the twins," Harold tells us, shaking his head.

Two days after learning of the affair, Sibille insisted that they break the news to the Streibels together. They agreed to meet at the Streibels' home, but when Sibille arrived, Frank had already left. He had been there earlier but had left in a hurry, without giving any explanation or revealing the intended reason behind the visit, Birgit remembers.

In her calm, unruffled way, Sibille took it upon herself to tell the Streibels about her husband's affair.

"We asked whether she intended to get a divorce. I could see the question had caught her off guard. 'No,' she had said, 'what about the children?' I think Sibille knew the Zanners' business affairs were under pressure and she would be anything but well off if she walked out of the marriage. She had no choice. She had to stay.

"But she was angry with Frank," says Birgit.

In due course, Sibille accepted Frank's child as an inevitable part of their lives. "She even began to think about a bigger car and about adding an extra room to the house for the little girl when she came on weekend visits."

Sibille was always optimistic, determined to see the positive side of things. It was as if she had simply decided to carry on with her life, Harold remembers. "She was prepared to give Frank a chance, on the condition that he broke off his relationship with Susanna."

The verdict is out as to whether Frank kept his end of the bargain. There were rumours that Frank had seen a lawyer about a divorce and had even begun to look for an apartment for Susanna and himself, the Streibels say.

The week before her death, they recall, Sibille was unusually quiet. "She wasn't herself," Birgit says. "We wondered whether she had given Frank an ultimatum. Or perhaps Susanna had insisted that Frank make a choice: either her or Sibille. Who will ever know?"

After our conversation, Piet and I walk with the Streibels up the steep driveway to the street. Three birches brought by them from Germany grow at the entrance to their property. A few metres away, our eyes automatically search out the place where Sibille was attacked.

On the pavement, the Streibels have laid out a small memorial garden. The Iceberg roses are in full bloom.

For Sibille.

25 September 2002. Flora Clinic, Roodepoort. Just before midnight.

Two men were standing between two large white columns at the entrance, smoking. They were strangers to each other. They didn't speak. Just smoked.

Both were waiting for news of their wives; both feared the worst.

Piet Byleveld had woken earlier that evening to discover his wife struggling to breathe beside him in bed. She was having heart problems.

Frank Zanner's wife lay with the arrow of a crossbow still lodged in her neck, frozen in the moment of the attack.

Now the two women lay in the intensive care unit, connected to tubes and monitors: the detective's wife, and the wife of the man whom the detective would later detain for her murder.

Outside, their husbands were smoking in silence.

Earlier that same evening the doctor had told the Streibels that there was no hope for Sibille. A machine was keeping her alive.

The Streibels remember how, when Frank heard the news, he turned away and threw his car keys across the room, his face distorted with sorrow.

The Streibels went to Frank's home to look after the twins for the night. It was very late when Frank returned from hospital. Birgit wanted to give him sugar-water for shock but he told her he hadn't eaten. She remembers thinking briefly that it was strange. Sibille always left him his supper, which he would eat as soon as he came home.

The next morning Frank said he was going to work. Surprised,

Birgit asked: Aren't you going to see Sibille? Aren't they going to switch off the machines?

"He told me, yes, he would go."

Later that morning the machines were switched off. Sibille died with the arrow still lodged in her neck.

The newspapers reported how Sibille's death sent shock waves through the German community. At her funeral, the St Thomas Lutheran Church in Bryanston was filled to capacity. There were family and friends from Europe, and people were sitting outside on the lawns to listen to the service. Frank gave Harold an envelope to place on Sibille's coffin.

Andrew Lloyd Webber's music filled the church: "Time to say goodbye." Frank began to cry inconsolably.

Captain Paula Nothnagel, police spokesperson at the West Rand, told the daily newspaper *Beeld* that the Zanner murder was one of the most bizarre murders the police had investigated for quite some time.

The motive for the murder was unknown. "We have nothing at this point, nothing. There are no suspects."

The police surmised that Sibille Zanner had known her attacker, because she appeared to have been walking towards her attacker before she was shot, *Beeld* reported.

Robbery had been excluded as a possible motive. Sibille's purse was full of cash. According to Nothnagel, the possibility of an assassination was being investigated.

A week later, after the autopsy had been completed, Nothnagel reported that Sibille had been shot at such close range that some of her hair had been found in the wound. The bolt had shattered her second neck vertebra and she had been instantly paralysed.

A weeping Frank told *Beeld* that the murder of his wife was a pathetic act. "She had no enemies. It's a complete mystery to me."

For seven months there was no progress with the investigation. A disgruntled Superintendent Bushie Engelbrecht withdrew the murder docket from the initial investigating officer, Captain Estelle Enslin. And then, on Friday 23 May 2003, just before it was time for his first Amstel of the weekend, Piet Byleveld took over Sibille Zanner's murder docket.

Roodepoort CAS 1496/09/02.

On Monday morning, Piet and Captain Mike van Aardt were sitting at Piet's desk, working through the docket. They were fed up, to put it mildly, Piet remembers.

"The crime scene had been handled extremely poorly, in a totally unacceptable manner. Sibille Zanner's handbag and other items lying in the street had not even been examined, had simply been tossed into her car. What about fingerprints?

"There was no photographer at the scene that night. Added to this, no one had taken proper statements from the first people on the scene. The investigation had been buggered up."

Piet had known nothing about the case before the docket landed on his desk. As he was bringing himself up to speed, he vaguely began to remember that night at the hospital and the man who had stood with him at the entrance, smoking, and talking constantly on his cellphone. "He'd seemed quite relaxed, I remembered, quite unemotional."

Back at his townhouse, Piet fetches a box of files from his garage. He searches until he finds a brown manilla envelope. A few photographs slide out. He arranges them, one by one, on the coffee table: Sibille Zanner's autopsy photos. They look almost surreal, like props staged for a movie – a macabre crime thriller.

The tip of the bolt is visible through the hair on one side, and the lime-green plastic vanes on the other side.

Piet had little to work with. There were no eyewitnesses. On the evening of the murder, Maria, the fifteen-year-old daughter of his colleague Superintendent Frikkie Page, who lives lower down in Marble Crescent, was returning from a shopping trip with her mother at about the time of the attack. She caught a glimpse of an approaching vehicle, driving almost in the middle of the road. She thought it might have been a white bakkie.

When she turned around and looked again, she saw someone lying in the street.

"Why was the bakkie driving in the middle of the road?" Piet wonders. "If it was because there was a body in the street, why didn't the driver stop? It was strange."

Plaster of Paris impressions of tyre tracks belonging to a 4×4 that had possibly stopped behind Sibille's car didn't reveal anything, Piet says.

It was a docket filled with questions, without any answers. Piet started by phoning Captain Estelle Enslin, the investigating officer he had replaced.

What could she tell him about Frank Zanner?

"She thought he was innocent. When I asked her how she knew this, she said her interviews with Zanner had convinced her that he wasn't the murderer."

Piet asked drily, isn't everyone a suspect until the right one has been arrested? He was definitely not excluding Frank Zanner.

"When Frank failed to pass a lie detector test, Enslin was no longer quite so convinced. Eddie Bezuidenhout, the ex-husband of Frank's sister, Corina, had been investigated by Enslin. But Eddie, who had allegedly sold Frank a crossbow, did pass a lie detector test."

As it happened, Piet didn't take much notice of the test results. They're not accepted by the courts anyway.

To his dismay, Piet began to suspect that Enslin and Frank Zanner had struck up a friendship. "If this was true, she couldn't

A police photo shows the bolt through Sibille Zanner's neck.

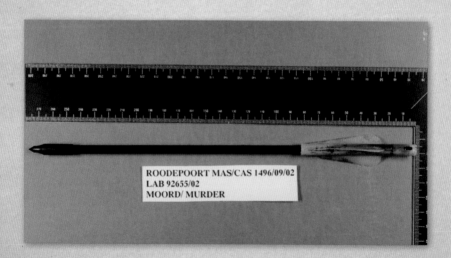

ROODEPOORT MAS/CAS 1496/09/02
LAB 92655/02
MOORD/ MURDER

A similar crossbow was used in the attack.

Sibille Zanner.

have been more out of line. As an investigating officer you must consider everyone a suspect or else you lose your objectivity."

Piet realised that there was no point in involving Enslin any further. "I was on my own. As usual."

And as usual, Piet did what he always does: he visited the scene of the crime – one which, seven months after the murder, was completely cold.

Up to that point, Piet had had no contact with Frank Zanner at all. He had deliberately avoided him because he wanted to focus his attention on Sibille.

"I wanted to know who she was, what she was, where she came from, what her movements were – every tiny detail about her."

From the first day it was clear that the case would not be an easy one. Piet found it especially difficult to access Sibille's friends and colleagues. "They were reluctant to talk to me and seemed not to trust me as a detective."

Her work was one of the first places that he visited. Everyone at Steinmüller told Piet how friendly and professional Sibille had been. The chief executive officer, Hein Spreitzer, described her as a "nice girl".

Then Piet heard about the mysterious telephone call.

A colleague, Victor Papenfus, told Piet that Sibille had been in a cheerful mood on the day of her death, until she'd received a phone call some time between noon and one o'clock. She had sounded very upset, Papenfus later testified in court. *Beeld* reported that he had heard her mention the name "Frank".

It was not like Sibille at all, Papenfus told Piet. In all the years he had known her, he had never seen her so upset. When he'd walked past her office to make sure she was all right, she had promptly switched to German on the phone.

Papenfus later looked in on her to try and cheer her up. She just said, "Men!" and shortly afterwards took her handbag and left. It was the last time he saw her alive.

Piet checked the phone records but couldn't establish the identity of her caller.

Who had Sibille's caller been? What had caused her outburst? Piet brooded over these questions for nights on end, sitting beside the fake-rock water feature in his garden, the homemade ashtray-on-a-stand close at hand.

"It's ironic that Sibille's admirable qualities of privacy and loyalty might have played some part in her demise. She might have been alive today if she had spoken to someone about her fears and problems."

Frank Zanner's financial position also raised some questions. There were rumours, Piet says, that, earlier that year, part of Paul Zanner's factory had been liquidated and that Frank had tried to increase his mortgage to acquire cash. It was also rumoured that, barely two days after Sibille's death, Frank had made inquiries to Steinmüller's book-keeper about the amount due to Sibille in her pension. At the time, the bookkeeper had found it strange, and now she told Piet.

Piet dug in his heels and ordered Steinmüller to stop any payments that they might consider giving to Frank. "Frank's attorneys tried to put pressure on me but I stuck to my guns."

On Piet's recommendation, and with an investigation pending, the insurance company refused to pay out an amount of R440 090 for a policy Zanner had taken out on Sibille's life, of which he was the sole beneficiary.

Four months after Sibille's death, Frank met Karen Wittmann through a mutual acquaintance. They went out together twice. Wittmann later testified in court that he had told her about his struggle to get Sibille's policy paid out. *Beeld* reported as follows: "He said the policy was worth only about a million rand but that it was still a million. All he said about his wife was that she had been a good cook and that people had liked her. He didn't seem crazy about her."

The more Piet learned about Sibille, the more he began to wonder whether she had, in fact, been able to make peace with her husband's deceit, no matter how hard she might have tried. Birgit told Piet that Sibille had always been adamant that she would forgive Frank for a one-night stand, but never for an affair.

As his investigation progressed, Piet began to suspect that Frank had confessed to Sibille only because he'd had no other choice. Sibille had been on the verge of finding out herself. At that point Susanna had broken off her relationship with Frank, although he apparently refused to let her go.

Michael Prescott, who had leased Susanna a cottage on his property in Honeydew between 2000 and 2003, told Piet about the violent arguments he'd overheard between Susanna and Frank. Apparently, Prescott had become fed up and warned Frank to stay away or he would tell his wife.

"Two days after Frank had confessed to Sibille, Prescott called on her to tell her about her husband's infidelity," Piet recalls. "She told him that she already knew."

Prescott later gave evidence in court about the "explosive" nature of the relationship between Frank and Susanna, describing the regular arguments between the two. Frank would call on her either very early in the morning or very late at night, Prescott said.

In August 2003, when Frank was arrested, Susanna moved out of the cottage and left the country. Prescott's wife, Debra, testified that Frank had phoned her after Susanna had left, in an attempt to discover her whereabouts. According to *Beeld*, Mrs Prescott said that even though she had an email address for Susanna she didn't give it to Frank because she didn't want to put the lives of Susanna and her daughter, Christina, "in danger".

Piet now changed his focus to the murder weapon. According to Eddie Bezuidenhout, he had sold Frank a crossbow and three arrows for R300 shortly before he moved to Germany in April 1992.

Later, Eddie told the court in detail how he had taken a box containing a crossbow from the boot of his green VW Golf and sold it to Frank. Eddie also mentioned Frank's love of karate and Chinese martial arts.

When Piet showed Eddie the arrow that had been in Sibille's neck, he denied that it was one of the arrows he had sold Frank.

Frank denied ever buying a crossbow from Eddie.

Susanna Hönigsperger was also not excluded as a suspect. She, after all, had reason to want Sibille out of the way.

In August 2003, Piet received an anonymous call: Susanna was packing. She was about to flee the country.

Piet jumped into his car and hurried to her place of work. At the main entrance, he was refused entry. He slipped in through a back door and caught Susanna in her office.

"She began to cry and said she was fleeing because she was afraid. Frank was threatening to take her child. He had even offered her money to sign the child over to his care."

Susanna left for Austria.

Finally Piet decided that his docket on Sibille Zanner and her life was comprehensive enough. It was time to zoom in on Frank.

The question was: could Frank have been at the scene of the crime?

Sibille was apparently killed outside the Streibels' home at 19:35. According to Frank's statement, he had arrived home at about 19:40. If that was true, it would rule him out as a suspect.

"The electronic entry card at Waterford Estate indicated, however, that he had entered at 19:54:45. The domestic help, Margaret

Lekgetho, said in a statement that the SABC2 soapie *Generations* had just started when Frank arrived home. I checked with the SABC. On 24 September, *Generations* started at 20:00 on the dot. Frank must therefore have come home just after eight.

"On 24 July 2003, Margaret said in a subsequent statement that Frank had told her she had made a mistake when she told the police the time he had come home. He was home earlier than that, but had worked out on his punchbag in the garage before coming inside. He had seen that the children were asleep, and Margaret had also been asleep in her chair. Margaret denied this. She had been in the kitchen, she insisted."

During the trial, Frank's neighbour, Brian Atkinson, stated that Frank had come to ask for his "help" a few months after the murder. *Beeld* reported that Zanner had "reminded" Atkinson and his wife of a conversation they were supposed to have had on the evening of the murder.

"During his visit, Zanner told us he was the chief suspect in his wife's murder and that we shouldn't be surprised if the police came to interview us," Atkinson testified. "He asked me whether I remembered seeing him in his driveway with his twin boys on the evening of the murder and asking him why they were up so late. I denied it. I didn't see him that night."

A question that haunted Piet was whether Frank could have committed the murder within the given time frame.

He and his team decided to re-enact Sibille's drive to the Streibels, thereby determining the time of the attack as accurately as possible. Afterwards they would do the same with the trip back to Waterford Estate, to determine whether it would have been possible for Frank to be back there at 19:54.

The entire exercise was performed according to legal requirements. Piet and Walter Hirzebruch, a police reservist acting as a witness, kept to the speed limits. They left Waterford Estate at

19:11, and at 19:31 sharp they stopped in front of the Streibels' home: a journey of nineteen kilometres, completed in twenty minutes, at an average speed of fifty-seven kilometres per hour.

They got out of the car. Piet lit a cigarette and showed Hirzebruch exactly where Sibille's body had been found. On the return trip, they decided to exceed the speed limit by twenty to thirty kilometres – something the attacker might well have done.

They left at 19:35, and at 19:52 they drew up at the Waterford Estate security gate, seventeen minutes later. Piet's simulated trips proved that Frank Zanner could have made the journey from the Streibels to Waterford Estate within the designated time frame.

The third trip they undertook was from Frank's workplace to the Streibel residence. Frank maintained that he had driven directly home from work. His time of departure, according to his statement, was 19:00. The drive home would therefore have taken him fifty-four minutes, according to the time of arrival on Waterford Estate's electronic entry card.

When Piet made this journey, it took only thirty-five minutes. However, when Piet drove from Zanner's workplace to the Streibel residence and then to Waterford Estate, the duration of the trip corresponded with the fifty-four minutes Zanner claimed to have spent driving home on the night Sibille was attacked.

"Frank could not explain the discrepancy. I realised with great clarity that it would have been perfectly possible for Frank to have killed his wife. It turned my mind, as we say in the police."

In September 2003, the Zanners employed the services of a private detective named Charles Landman, one of Piet's ex-colleagues, a former commander at Brixton Murder and Robbery.

Piet laughs. "It was their attempt to establish an alibi for Zanner. Well … they put it differently: to investigate Zanner's alibi."

A reconstruction of the murder scene.

Landman later told *Beeld* he had been asked to follow up and investigate Frank's alibi – not to fabricate one for him.

Out of the blue, Landman phoned Piet and gave him a tip: examine the access-control security camera at Zanner's factory to determine the exact time Frank had left the premises. "But when I followed it up, the camera was suddenly missing."

It was like a game between two detectives. Here's something you haven't thought of but, hey, you're too late, the tracks have been erased.

At last, on 28 August 2003, Piet decided it was time for blue lights and handcuffs – it was time to arrest Frank Zanner. In Piet's usual manner, it could be summed up in two words: surprise and intimidation.

For a moment Piet sets aside the Zanner case and focuses on those blue police lights, at that Moment of Arrest.

"The lights show I'm in control. The adrenalin pumps. Tremendously. Man, I'm telling you, nothing beats that feeling. Not even sex."

He grins. "You know you're going to swoop at any moment and arrest the man. You know the end is near. Not the ultimate end, of course, that's when sentencing takes place in court, but you're going to unmask the man."

Piet had found out the exact time Zanner usually left for work and which route he followed, and he had decided on an appropriate spot to arrest him. So the cops were waiting outside the gates of Waterford Estate at six-fifteen in the morning, with Piet and Mike van Aardt in one vehicle, and Ronnie Magina and Lucky Ramaboea in another.

Shortly after half past six Frank Zanner left the complex. Piet put the blue light on the roof of the vehicle and they cut Zanner off with great fanfare, forcing him off the road when he failed to stop immediately.

Piet jumped out, his 9-mill trained on Zanner.

Overkill, perhaps?

"I had to, I knew he could be armed. The surprise element, ma'am!

"But, more important, I wanted to study his reaction. All he said was, 'Is it really necessary to arrest me like this?' Nothing else." Zanner speaks with a slight lisp, Piet remembers.

It was music to Piet's own ears when he spoke the words, "I'm arresting you for the murder of Sibille Zanner."

Zanner was shocked. Piet could see he hadn't been expecting it.

"There was a strange look on his face. I made him get out of his vehicle, cuffed and shackled him and searched his vehicle. On our way to the charge office we didn't say a word to him."

Zanner's vehicle was photographed so that Maria Page, the girl who might have seen a white bakkie in Marble Crescent just after the attack, could look at the photos with a view to a possible identification.

Piet remembers that when Zanner was brought to Piet's office for questioning, he was arrogant. "He sat with his hands behind his head.

"'Who do you think you are?' he asked me. And then he added: 'I want my lawyer.'"

But Piet was not to be intimidated. "Listen," he said, "who the hell do you think you're talking to? You're not in your father's office or your mansion now! Neither are you dealing with the wife you killed."

Piet continues: "I won't allow anyone to patronise me. I'm willing to communicate with him but he mustn't try to intimidate me. It makes me angry.

"Then I tried a new tactic: I showed Zanner a photo of his late wife. He refused to look. He couldn't face it. It's like a game of chess – I love it."

Then Piet made Zanner stand in his office for a good hour and a half. When he wanted to sit down, Piet instructed Ronnie and Lucky to hold him up.

"He was angry but said nothing; he restrained himself."

When they allowed him to make the telephone call he was entitled to, Frank phoned his mother. She contacted his lawyer cousin, Richard Zanner, who, in turn, sent for Advocate Danie Dörfling. "An ace sc," Piet calls him.

Two aces facing off: Gerrit Roberts for the state and Danie Dörfling for the defence.

The next morning Zanner's warning statement was taken down in Dörfling's presence, with an accompanying note by Captain van Aardt: "… white male, dressed in long trousers and shirt, appears to be relaxed and within his full senses."

Zanner reacted to every question, even the simplest, with: "I'll consult on that." There were pages filled with questions, followed by, "I'll consult …" His thumb print and signature were at the bottom.

In front of him, Piet knew, sat a hard nut.

But Zanner sat facing another hard nut.

"I'm sure he had a hard time in prison. You're in that airless cell almost twenty-three hours a day, in the company of twenty-odd murderers, armed robbers, rapists – all together. They have no mercy. I could see he'd lost weight in the few months before he was granted bail. Frank Zanner certainly didn't sit down to eisbein and sauerkraut in prison, believe me. It's dip and porridge. You dip your porridge in a little sauce and then you eat. And dry bread and coffee, or sometimes bread and a little butter. And for supper there might be some watered-down chicken broth."

The next time Piet saw Zanner was in court.

"When bail was refused with the first application, I could see that the last bit of fight had gone out of Frank Zanner."

Piet Byleveld didn't take the *Sowetan* and a Bar-One to Zanner's cell. Or a radio. Neither did he share a braai with him beside the highway. Or talk about soccer in an attempt to get inside his head.

On 31 October 2003, Zanner appealed in the Johannesburg High Court and was released on bail of R30 000. His sons were returned to his care.

In the meantime, Piet had taken out of mothballs a thirteen-year-old case in which Frank Zanner had been implicated but not charged.

"On 12 March 1992, Zanner had thrown a vernier gauge [a measuring tool] at an employee at SA Linishers, the Zanners' factory in Chamdor, Krugersdorp." Samuel Tumisang Segaetso (50) later died in the Main Reef Hospital.

"In both Sibille and Sam's deaths unusual objects had been used as the murder weapon."

In 1993, the police investigated a case of culpable homicide against Zanner. During the inquest, on 8 March 1993, the magistrate, Mr IM Taylor of Krugersdorp, was unable to make a ruling and it was decided not to charge Frank Zanner.

"We traced two further witnesses and I found enough evidence to charge him. At the time of the first investigation the eyewitness had not been able to testify because the case was never heard in court. I obtained a new statement from Inspector Ben Booysen, the investigating officer, who declared that it had been a case 'where everything was not quite as it should be and where I felt that the accused and the witnesses were keeping information from me'."

Piet and his team also obtained a statement from a former employee of SA Linishers, Cornelius Jacob Badenhorst, who, *Beeld* reported, alleged that Zanner was a "pig" with a "very short temper". The defence objected against this statement.

When Piet felt that they stood a chance of having Zanner convicted at least of culpable homicide, he took his dockets to

Advocate Gerrit Roberts. "He looked at the Segaetso case and said: 'Piet, go ahead.'"

In June 2004, Frank Zanner was charged with Segaetso's murder.

Advocate Gerrit Roberts said in his statement that it was clear at the time that a prima facie case existed against Zanner.

Zanner's legal team's application for the charge to be withdrawn was rejected by the High Court. An appeal was noted, but the Court of Appeal ruled that the state could proceed with a second murder charge.

"We spent weeks and weeks in court before the trial even began. It was nerve-wracking. Exhausting."

At that stage, Piet was also in the middle of the Sipho Dube trial. He literally had to jog between Courts 2A (Zanner) and 2F (Dube) – fortunately both on the same floor.

"I knew I had Sipho. But not Zanner."

Piet had two weeks to prepare the statements for the Frank Zanner trial.

On 26 July 2004, Frank Zanner stood trial for the murders of Samuel Segaetso (Count 1) and Sibille Zanner (Count 2).

The two counts were being heard simultaneously and Judge Joop Labuschagne would deliver judgment on both at the end of the trial.

The vernier gauge case came up first. The eyewitness, Martha Tshigalo, testified that she had seen Frank throw the vernier gauge at another employee, Tony Picota, in anger, after he had called Tony three times. They had argued shortly before the incident. The vernier had missed Picota but struck "Uncle Sam", Tshigalo stated.

"Frank ran to Uncle Sam, grabbed him before he hit the ground and pulled the vernier out of his head."

"Tshigalo was an excellent witness," Piet says. "After her testimony I was hopeful."

The police officer who had been involved at the time, Booysen, took a hammering during cross-examination, Piet says. "He was given a hard time because he couldn't remember anything that well. But it was thirteen years ago. Besides, the original docket on Segaetso's death had disappeared, together with Booysen's original statement.

"To crown it all, it was alleged that the vernier had 'slipped' out of Zanner's hand ..."

Then the crossbow case started.

Piet was still optimistic. He had a good case, he believed. His preparation had been thorough. His witnesses had been prepped. He was going to wipe the floor with Frank Zanner.

Advocate Roberts said in his statement that he had taken the decision to prosecute based on strong circumstantial evidence, which the state is entitled to do.

Then the wheels came off. Piet's witnesses crumbled. "It turned into a nightmare. During the bail application, five judges had found that we had a case, but in this court ..."

Maria Page, who had seen the vehicle at the crime scene, could not identify the bakkie without a shadow of a doubt. And her mother, Renee, had a hard time during cross-examination.

It was clear to the court that the Pages could not have seen much of the suspect vehicle that night.

What undermined his case was that no photographs had been taken at the crime scene, Piet explains. "That was the first mistake. The fact that we had reconstructed the scene and that the legal teams and the judge had visited it could not compensate for that."

Susanna Hönigsperger was on standby in Austria for the duration of the trial. "Though I was disappointed when the prosecutor decided not to call her as a witness, I think the defence would have discredited her evidence in any event."

He's quiet for a moment, his finger rubbing the side of his nose.

Atkinson, Zanner's neighbour, was no longer sure of the time that Zanner had arrived home. And just before the Zanners' domestic help, Margaret, was due to be called to the stand, she changed her version of the events. "She maintained that I had told her what to write in her statement. We decided not to call her as a witness, as it was likely that she'd have harmed our case further."

Piet had obtained a statement from Eddie Bezuidenhout's brother, Tony, in England, in which he claimed to have been present when the crossbow was sold to Frank. Eddie was a fiasco in the courtroom, Piet says. "Advocate Dörfling delved into his past and branded him as 'deceitful, untruthful and aggressive'. It was clear to me that it would be useless to have Tony come from England to testify."

He shakes his head despondently.

"It was a very strange case. Nothing was in my favour, everything was against me … Everything that could possibly go wrong, went wrong for Sibille Zanner …"

The testimony of Professor Hendrik Scholtz, forensic pathologist and head of the Department of Forensic Medicine at the University of the Witwatersrand, made headlines.

The immense force with which the bolt had penetrated Sibille's neck indicated that it had been fired from a crossbow rather than driven into her neck by hand, Professor Scholtz stated. The bolt had entered under her right ear and penetrated the thick ligaments between the first two vertebrae, which had left her instantly paralysed.

"Initially the professor thought that the bolt might have been driven through the neck by hand. We argued the point for an hour. He isn't an expert in the field. I am."

At last Piet's case hung by a single thread: the reliability of the access-control equipment used at Waterford Estate.

"There was one problem," he says, "I didn't have the video material showing the exact time Zanner had left the factory."

Piet summoned the engineers from Cape Town who had developed the software and installed the access-control equipment at Waterford Estate.

"They were supposed to testify about the credibility and precision of their equipment. Their initial testimony was excellent but under cross-examination they admitted that something might have gone wrong with the instruments. After that, I could no longer use our finely constructed simulated trip as evidence.

"So … when the access-control evidence collapsed, I knew we were in trouble."

Advocate Dörfling applied for acquittal by maintaining that the state had failed to prove Zanner had lied about not being at home on the evening of his wife's attack. Zanner, it was alleged, had had no motive for killing his wife. On the contrary, she had accepted her husband's infidelity.

On 1 August 2006, the state dropped the charge against Zanner on the first murder count – that he had shot and killed his wife. "The state admitted that, although many of his actions had been suspect, there was insufficient evidence for a reasonable man to find the accused guilty," Advocate Roberts said.

On 4 August, a tearful Frank Zanner was acquitted on the second murder count – that of murdering Segaetso. Judge Joop Labuschagne granted Zanner's application for acquittal. "I find that there is no evidence that the accused had any intention to murder the deceased. There is, however, no doubt that he acted negligently. He is an educated, intelligent man," the judge said.

As he listened to Judge Joop Labuschagne reading his judgment, Piet lowered his head. "To the ground. One feels …"

Three years after being charged, Zanner walked down the courtroom steps a free man.

The biggest disappointment of his career, Piet calls it.

"It was the first case I ever lost in the High Court. But I can't blame the judge. Not at all. The witnesses dropped us."

But who grabbed Sibille Zanner that evening in Marble Crescent and shot an arrow through her neck? Who killed Sibille Zanner?

Piet doesn't say anything. He just looks at me.

As was the custom, Piet took the state's legal team to dinner on the evening after the judgment. They were a sorry lot. "They were just as shattered as I was. And that was that. That's all I can tell you."

In 2007, Piet was in a shopping mall in Centurion when he heard someone shout: "Byleveld!"

It was Frank Zanner. Piet just looked at him.

"He asked what I was doing. I told him it was none of his business. 'And don't shout at me', I told him. 'If you don't approach me professionally, I won't speak to you.' Then I turned away and sat down. He was being friendly. I wasn't."

In 2010, the *Cape Argus* reported that Frank Zanner was suing the state for R8,5 million in general damages for harm to his reputation and rights, for harming his honour and dignity, for the associated inconvenience, and for humiliation and mental and bodily harm because of emotional shock, angst and depression resulting from his arrest and the fact that there had been no reasonable belief in the truth of the charges laid against him.

He accused Piet Byleveld of sloppy investigation work.

In another development, Zanner's claims of R2 million against two pension funds, both in Sibille's name, were rejected. The two companies had created trust funds for the Zanners' adopted twin sons after Zanner went to trial. In 2007, a year after he was acquitted, Zanner disputed the companies' right to set up a trust fund without his consent. The money is still in trust.

When he thinks of Sibille today, Piet still feels he has let her down. "Somewhere I might have done something wrong, overlooked something. At first I thought about it endlessly, trying to establish where I had gone wrong, even though I knew there was nothing more I could have done. I suppose I was trying to find peace of mind.

"I do believe I went as far as I could. As I do with every case."

He taps with his finger on two thick dockets. His face is flushed.

"I didn't succeed … And now it's over. I have to make peace with it. But whenever I think about it, everything comes back. The disappointment and anger. But it's no good clinging to the past. There are many things in the future, many victims that deserve my attention."

And the other critical patient in the Flora Clinic that evening when Sibille was admitted – Esmie Byleveld?

"That evening in hospital I felt really sorry for her. She almost didn't make it."

Initially she recovered well. Four days after being admitted she was discharged, but a week later she had a setback. And another. Her recovery was slow. She had to get a pacemaker and her vision was impaired.

She did manage to adapt to her new circumstances, but her horizons had shrunk. Piet had to take over responsibility for the entire household, and care for her fully. He was under greater pressure than ever.

PIED PIPER OF THE MINE DUMPS

"I have two cellphones. If you sell them, part of the money is yours."

The woman considers the proposal. She doesn't know the filthy little man, but her income from the clothes she sells on a Saturday morning here in Jules Street, Malvern, is meagre.

"I work just around the corner. The children can come with me to fetch the phones," he suggests.

"Go along," the woman tells the two cousins, aged ten and eleven, who are helping her today. She's the aunt of the eleven-year-old – the one that still looks like a little girl, with dimples in her apple cheeks.

When they have walked a short distance, the younger child begins to feel uneasy. The man smells of alcohol. She pulls her cousin aside. Let's rather go back, she tries to convince her. No, her cousin says, I have to go, my aunt told me to.

The younger one stays behind, hovering uncertainly. When she looks for her cousin again, she and the man have disappeared around a corner. She turns and goes back to her aunt.

The man has a firm grip on the child's hand. They walk past the last buildings, up the slope of a mine dump.

He throws her onto the ground, suddenly aggressive, pulls down her shorts, picks up a stone and hits her in the face. He finds more stones, as big as four, five bricks, stands over her and throws them with brute force onto her face. She tries to protect herself with her hands, but they are also smashed. He severs the middle finger of her left hand and pockets his macabre loot.

He walks away. In the grass behind him lies the broken body of an obedient little girl who had listened to her aunt. Only eleven years old.

On 12 November 2003, Director Charles Johnson summoned Piet and handed him his next docket full of problems: Jeppe CAS 478/11/2003. Another serial killer.

This time it was obviously a paedophile that targeted young children and lured them away, like the Pied Piper of Hamelin.

Piet was instantly sucked in.

January 2010. We are standing in the wind next to a mine dump at Jeppe, close to the M2 freeway. Wemmer Pan is just around the corner. It is a bleak landscape, dug up, used, discarded. It is the hunting ground of Johannesburg South, the lair of serial killers.

The tradition started in the 1920s, when Daisy de Melker walked into a pharmacy in Turffontein to buy some arsenic with which she later disposed of two of her husbands and her son.

Seventy years later, the south's serial killers have become even crueller and more productive: Moses Sithole, David Selepe, Lazarus Mazingane, Cedric Maake, Sipho Dube … Why so many murderers have originated from this area remains a mystery.

Dust whirls around our legs. Piet and I are standing against his car, our backs against the wind. His Mercedes will definitely need a wash after this excursion.

"I've flattened every blade of grass here following my various clients. Not once, not twice, many times, I'm telling you."

Piet's mind shifts away from murders and mine dumps, and I am allowed a rare glimpse of his inner self.

"For years I trusted no one. I showed no one who Piet Byleveld was; no one besides my own family knew anything about me. I blundered along between cases. For years and years. In time I no longer knew who I was myself."

Piet was jaded, numb to a point where Amstels and Grandpas no longer helped. All he had were his two little dogs and the Blue Bulls. And *7de Laan*, when he got the chance to watch.

All that really mattered were his cases. Guilty verdicts. The only people he connected with were his clients. Murderers.

Behind the facebrick walls of his townhouse in Weltevreden Park the situation had become pretty grim in the wake of Esmie's heart problems in 2002. "She was totally dependent on me. I even shopped for her clothes and toiletries."

Photographs of Piet taken at the time show a stoic man who, pale-faced, emotionless, was clearly overworked. A man turned into himself, old beyond his years.

But that was not what the public saw. With five serial-killing successes behind him, Piet Byleveld had a large fan base, especially among black South Africans, as someone who solved cases in areas neglected by detectives in the past: townships and poor rural areas.

Stress at home, success at work – that was Piet's life when Jeppe CAS 478/11/2003 landed on his desk.

This time the suspect had already been apprehended by members of the public.

When Piet received the docket of Mthandeni Sipho Matthews Hlangathi Dube he had been charged with a single murder: that of eleven-year-old Tina Bernardes.

Though his client was behind bars, Piet instinctively knew that more bodies lay buried under stones somewhere. He wanted to have Dube charged as a serial killer, but to do that he would have to positively link him to more killings – and to do that he would need the man to confess.

Piet realised that his ability to squeeze a confession out of an unwilling detainee would be sorely tested with Sipho Dube. Piet has quite a reputation in the police for getting suspects to talk. When none of his colleagues had been able to get the child rapist Fanwell Khumalo to confess they had asked Piet to have a go at him. Piet was not the investigating officer. He still laughs when he remembers how, during the interview with Khumalo, he ranted: "I'm sick and tired of your lies. I'm going to drink a beer so that I can calm down."

When Piet returned, Khumalo talked.

This talent spills over into his personal life. He is seldom wrong with his judgment of people, and people are often uneasy in his company. He'll give you a sidelong glance and ask a few subtle questions to which he already knows the answers.

Piet's cellphone rings and he gets back into the car to escape the wind. It's the press. They want him to comment. He makes a few trite, official remarks. He ends the converation, looks up and says: "I thrive under pressure, actually. Put me under pressure, I'm mad about it. I function better when I simply have to cope, see?"

Operation Dube. Piet gathered his team – Captain Mike van Aardt and Inspectors Shezi, Magina and Ramaboea. The Unit for Serious and Violent Crimes was stationed at Alexandra police station after Brixton Murder and Robbery, together with other specialist units, had been abolished in 2000. Dube was being detained at the Sophiatown police station.

Piet will never forget their first meeting. "This small fellow stood in front of me, in handcuffs and shackles. Short. Filthy. Stinking. A homeless person. He had scars on his face and a pert goatee. His smell almost made me long for Maake, Mazingane and Mfeka. Serial killers are usually quite neat, and generally big on personal hygiene. They can hold down jobs, they are 'normal' citizens."

Sipho Dube, on the other hand, was a phantom. He had no ID, his birth had never been registered, his fingerprints were not in the system, and he had no fixed address.

"Nothing, can you believe it? It was as if he didn't exist. He was homeless. He slept in the veld or under flyovers on the highway; he rummaged in garbage bins for cigarette butts.

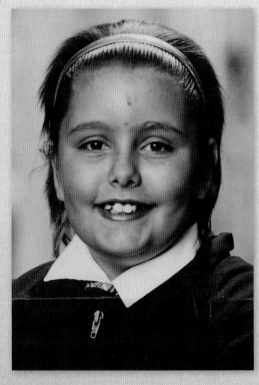

Tina Bernardes (left) and her parents, Tino and Jacky Bernardes.

"An outcast who survived by selling scrap. As a hobby he killed children in his spare time.

"I could see in his face there was something wrong with him. There was a wild expression in his eyes. You could sense his temper seething just below the surface."

This temper Piet would later experience first-hand.

Dube refused to communicate at all. During that entire first meeting he didn't make eye contact with Piet even once. All he did was growl.

"I'm serious – Dube would growl like an animal."

It was only during their third meeting that Piet managed to get through to him. Kind of. Cigarettes opened the way to Dube's heart. He went around picking up cigarette butts, sucking them without lighting them. Cigarettes became Piet's bait. Talk to me, he told Dube, and I'll see that you get smokes.

Dube refused to eat as well. When Piet bought him food yet again and he refused to eat it Piet lost his temper and tossed the food into a garbage bin. Highly indignant, Dube pleaded with Piet to take his food out of the bin. For Piet, it felt like a breakthrough.

Later he managed to convince Dube to shower more often. The other prisoners in the cells complained about his smell. Piet gave him some of his old suits, shoes and shirts. "At least you'll look respectable in court," Piet said to him. The subtext was: I'm looking after you, Sipho, so … co-operate.

Piet begins to laugh. "No, look, this fellow was a strange customer!"

But this scumbag taught Piet one important lesson: endless patience.

"Look, there are always hours of consultations with serial killers. If you show your impatience that connection of trust between the two of you is damaged and the entire investigation is set back. But Sipho had my nerves frazzled."

For Piet, with his restless nature, unable to sit still for ten minutes without getting bored, getting what he needed from Dube was a learning curve.

On Sunday 16 November, during their third interview in Alexandra, Dube admitted he had killed Tina Bernardes. He was even willing to point out the murder scene. Things were coming to a head. Piet rewarded Dube with chips and white bread for lunch. "And milk. I had found out that he was mad about milk. And a cigarette for dessert."

Besides the Bernardes murder scene, Dube also pointed out a house in Queen Street, Mayfair, where he had kidnapped two cousins, Anele (9) and Siyabonga Mbuku (12), before killing them elsewhere. The police never found the bodies.

The dirty Pied Piper of the mine dumps had lured the two cousins to their death with a plastic Rambo figurine.

Anele and Siyabonga had arrived at the house of Anele's mother, Sophie, in the company of Dube, who supposedly wanted to sell them the Rambo figurine. Sophie told Dube she had no money and asked him to leave.

Some time later, under the impression that Dube had left, Sophie sent the two boys on an errand to her sister's house, a short distance away. After a while she went in search of them and found them in Dube's company again. She threatened him with the police if he didn't leave the children alone. She entered her house and when she came out five minutes later, Dube was missing. As were the two boys. For ever.

After Dube had pointed out the two murder sites, Piet sat studying his notes late into the night. It was quiet in the unit. Everyone else had long since gone home. All the information, in neat plastic pockets, was fixed to his office walls with Prestik. Step by step, the murder organogram was evolving.

Tina Bernardes was abducted on 8 November 2003 after her aunt, Maria Johnson, had sent her and her cousin with Dube to fetch two cellphones.

Shrewdly, feigning concern about the children's safety, Dube had even suggested that they bring a bag so that the phones would not be visible and make them a target for robbery.

When Tina failed to return, her family searched for her all through the night. They made a huge effort to find her. Her uncle, Joaquim, distributed hundreds of pamphlets with her photograph on them. The entire community helped search for her.

A homeless man, Alfred Nyanga, told Tina's father he had seen Dube walk hand in hand into the bushes with a little white girl. Nyanga had recognised Dube because he often ran into him at the scrapyard in Eloff Street. Nyanga lived under the bridge at the M2 east off-ramp.

Tino Bernardes, Tina's father, gave Nyanga R50 and asked him to phone him the minute he saw Dube again. The next morning Bernardes got the call: Dube was at the scrapyard. Tino and Joaquim hurried there, and Nyanga pointed Dube out to them. At first, Dube tried to convince them that he didn't have anything to do with Tina's disappearance, but they bundled him into the car and took him to Maria Johnson. When she confirmed that he was the man with whom Tina had left they handed him over to the police.

That same day Tina's body was found on a mine dump in Jeppe, near the Denver off-ramp on the M2.

The crime-scene photographs show the bloodied stones used in the attack still lying next to the crumpled body.

"Look at the blood on the grass. It shows how vicious the attack was."

Piet suspected that the Bernardes family blamed Maria Johnson for allowing Tina to walk off with a strange man. When she testified in court no one in the family said a word to her.

After Dube was caught, Alfred Nyanga, who, as a result of his positive identification of the man, had undoubtedly prevented many other children from ending up as Dube's prey, vanished into thin air. When Piet went looking for him to put him on the stand, he was missing. An extensive search led nowhere.

Perhaps he was afraid Dube's sangoma mother would put a spell on him, Piet speculates. In the past, he had often been seen around Jeppe, where Dube's mother lived.

Tina's parents told *Beeld* that it would have been their daughter's first visit to the seaside in December. She had been very excited when she'd received her first beach towel. Three years after Tina's death her parents still wept bitterly whenever they spoke of their only child.

Tina used to laugh all the time; she was a sweet, gentle child, her mother, Jacky, said. To make matters worse, Tino lost his job when he stayed away from work on the day of Tina's funeral.

According to Jacky, Tino at first took out his anger and frustration on the plates in their kitchen but then he started gardening to keep his hands and mind busy, and created a memorial garden for Tina.

"I feel so sorry for them," Piet says. "Children are always … to lose a child … it's difficult."

It's in the way he handles the victims' relatives that Piet, the aspirant pastor of the Waterberg, comes to the fore. He delivers the bad tidings in the most proper and gentlemanly way possible, as only he can. He concludes by saying: "I can't tell you why these things happen. But I assure you I won't rest until I catch the person who did this to your loved one." He offers them a way to take a step back from the emotion and focus their thoughts elsewhere: on the fact that the perpetrator is going to be caught. Something will be done. "In most cases it's enough to give the next of kin a small measure of comfort.

"I give them the assurance: I'm available twenty-four hours

a day. Phone me." In time, he automatically becomes the link between the many witnesses involved with the trial; they know they can rely on him.

Besides Tina Bernardes and the Mbuku cousins, Dube told Piet about other murders. Piet studied numerous dockets of unsolved murders in the area and began cross-referencing between Dube's stories and these dockets.

One that matched Dube's confessions was the case of fourteen-year-old Nomnikelo Juma, who disappeared on 6 August 2003 while walking home from her school in Soweto. Her body was later found in Bertrams, with stab wounds in the neck and under one armpit. The semen found on her slacks was ultimately the only DNA that could be connected with Dube. Finally, Piet could sleep better at night. Now he had strong evidence and not mere shaky confessions.

Dube pointed out several scenes for which Piet and his team could find no dockets. Sometimes Dube seemed confused during these excursions. Some of the murders had been committed while he was under the influence of alcohol.

Dube admitted openly that he didn't know the exact number of people he had killed.

Oddly, Piet says, serial killers are often relieved when they are finally caught and are able to confess. "They feel cleansed of the burden and immediately become more amiable towards me."

Furthermore, they appear bizarrely proud of their actions and tend to boast about their feats. They seem to consider Piet as a partner. But later, in court, when reality hits home, they give Piet and the other policemen a very hard time. They will say anything to get out of the situation they are in. Maake, Mazingane and Themba Nkosi threatened and swore at Piet in court. But Dube was the worst.

On Christmas Eve, Piet received a call from the Sandton police station. He must come at once, he was told. His suspect has lost his marbles.

He rushed over, bracing himself for another session of flying faeces. But Dube had a different tactic from that of Maake and Mazingane.

Dube had blocked the plug hole of the wash basin in his cell with clothing, opened the taps and flooded his cell. Piet battled until four that morning to calm him down.

"When he threw a tantrum like that you might as well leave him. His voice turned into a growl, like that of an animal. Look, I struggled with that man. It was rough at times."

To top it all, after he had calmed down, Dube asked Piet sweetly for a Zulu Bible. One day he was going to be a pastor, didn't Piet know?

Piet shakes his head. Dube's dual personality was fascinating: filthy and charming, Christian and killer. A mixture of love and hatred towards his mother.

Like all his other serial-killer clients Dube had a thing about his mother. Mother Mavis, the muti doctor from Jeppe.

"He wanted to see her with all his might but when I took him there, he lost control and cursed her terribly, blaming her for all the murders he had committed."

"She put a spell on me, that's why," Dube once almost pleadingly tried to explain to Piet. Dube had even brought his mother the body parts of some of the children he had killed. It was a bizarre and grisly partnership.

Piet frowns.

"And next thing I know, he escapes from custody …"

No one except the investigating team was allowed to book Dube out of the Alexandra police station. However, on 13 January 2004,

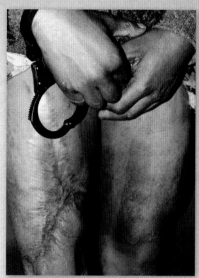

Sipho Dube. The scars from the bus accident are clearly visible.

A young survivor pointing out the scene where she was attacked.

the uniform branch inexplicably sent him to the Wynberg court, near Alexandra.

"It was an admin error; he should never have been there. Even worse, when they discovered that he wasn't on the court roll, they told him he was free to go. Dube casually walked out, dressed in one of the suits I had given him."

When Piet arrived the following morning to book Dube out for further identification of murder scenes he heard that Dube had been taken to court the previous day and had subsequently vanished into thin air. Piet was livid. Alexandra's officers saw a different side of him that day.

The police members who were responsible for the security lapse were later charged with negligence. There was now immense pressure on Piet from his seniors. The whole situation was an incredible embarrassment to him, and he felt that his colleagues had let him down.

Worse, it was not the first time that Dube had made the police look like fools. Before he had been arrested, he had sometimes posed as a concerned member of the public and offered his services to the police at the scenes of the murders he had committed.

At the scene of Nomnikelo Juma's murder, for instance, the police's suspicions had not been raised even when Dube had led them up the hill to Nomnikelo's blood-soaked school blazer and books. He had even described to the investigating officers how she had been raped and had run down the hill before falling down dead. And he had had the audacity to tick the police off for failing to do their jobs properly. They were so inattentive that they failed to notice the blood on Dube's shoes.

"Bloody hell," says Piet, clearly annoyed, "such arrogance! And such sloppy police work!"

But in the wake of Dube's escape, Piet was beside himself. He knew Dube would already be on the prowl. He was going to kill more children.

"His mother supposedly helped in the search for him. 'Corrupt' is written in large letters on that woman's forehead. She led us by the nose, even sent us all the way to KwaZulu-Natal, where we hung around for five, six days. She had a nice little holiday at the police's expense. A complete waste of time."

At last, three months later, things started to look up when Piet got an anonymous tip that Dube had been arrested for attempted car theft and assault in the Cleveland police district. He had been booked under a false name: Clifford Mbatha.

Just four days after he had escaped, Dube had tried to steal a car, but, unfortunately for him, he had chosen the wrong man's car. When Bradley Adams came out to see why his car alarm had gone off Dube and two accomplices fled down the street. Not the kind of man to leave it at that, Adams had followed in hot pursuit. Eventually Dube got tired and plonked himself down on the pavement. When Adams confronted him, Dube tried to stab him with a knife, inflicting a flesh wound. Adams overpowered him and took him to the Cleveland police station.

Piet laughs and says, "Luckily for Adams, he didn't know he had apprehended a dangerous serial killer!"

It took a whole three months before Piet got the anonymous tip. In the Cleveland police station's investigation diary Piet spotted the number Clifford Mbata had given as his mother's cell number. It was exactly the same number as Dube's mother's number. Again those eyes had not missed a thing.

"It was an immense relief, to put it mildly, ma'am!"

When Piet tracked down Dube in the Johannesburg prison, Dube grinned and said: "I'm sorry, Mister Piet." He told Piet with great relish how the policemen had held open the courtroom doors for him so that he could walk out free. Later he phoned Piet and said: "Mister Piet, there are more places. I want to show them to you because I trust you."

Sipho Dube trusted someone, possibly for the first time in his life.

Together they climbed mine dumps, crossed open tracts of veld, and walked along lonely footpaths, following Sipho Dube's bloody trail of ruined children's lives.

Dube also told Piet how he had blatantly phoned the parents of a victim he had just murdered: "Hello. My name is Sipho," he had said. "Your son Thabo is dead."

This was after he had sodomised and strangled the poor child, stoned him and cut off his arms as muti for his mother. Dube phoned Thabo's mother a second time, and said she should tell her husband to forget about his son.

Twelve days after Thabo's disappearance, the decomposed body of a child was found only a few kilometres from his home, but the police failed to connect it with Thabo's disappearance.

After Dube had accompanied the police to the scene, Captain Mike van Aardt went through the case dockets. The dead child was indeed Thabo.

"Two years after his disappearance, his parents received the news that their son's body had been found. They identified his clothing – red, blue and yellow shorts and brown sandals – from the police photographs."

Piet and his men set off for Dube's place of birth in Mhlumayo, a mountainous rural area near Ladysmith.

For the first time Piet could form a complete picture of Sipho Dube's psyche. His aunt told Piet that young Sipho had been out of control even at an early age. At seven he had stolen a neighbour's radio and, as a bonus, the altar money from the church. His mother had kicked him out of the house and he had gone to live with his grandmother. Piet could not establish who his father was.

At the Mhlumayo Primary School, his teachers had been forever at their wits' end with the child. His nickname had been Ndoji – truant player. He had seemed intelligent and spoken perfect English, but had caused trouble wherever he went. In grade five he had been expelled, according to www.documentingreality.com.

To make matters worse, young Sipho was run over by a bus. He was nearly killed and spent four months in hospital. The scars were still visible on his legs. The bus accident seemed to derail him even further.

He waged a mini reign of terror on the neighbourhood, looting the neighbours' homes. The other children were dead scared of him. Dube was angry with everyone, angry with everything. He was an outcast whom everyone avoided, his aunt said.

"She had a soft spot for him and thought at first that he was being falsely accused. When she heard what Dube was being charged with, however, she was shocked into silence."

Every serial killer seems to have his own particular fetish. Lazarus Mazingane had his uniquely knotted rope and Cedric Maake his shoe collection. Sipho Dube prayed. If the prayer was a good one then it was a sign that he shouldn't kill the child. A bad prayer would result in stones raining down on the unfortunate young victim.

His first sexual experience had been at a very young age when a homosexual man forced him to have sex, or rather, simulated sex, by shoving his penis between Dube's legs. Perhaps a deep-seated anger about this incident made him choose children as his victims. When asked in court why he preferred to prey on children, Dube said, "There's a difference between children and adults. Children belong to God."

Dube's criminal career started in 1997 when he was sentenced to eighteen months in the Ladysmith prison for attempted theft. He had scarcely been released when he was back in prison in 1999, this time for housebreaking. In 2000, after he had raped a little girl, he fled the area.

The confessions didn't stop.

"Mister Piet, I killed someone in Ladysmith too," Dube said, and he offered to take Piet to the scene.

On 23 March 2001, Rashunthee Singh, a thirty-eight-year-old widow and mother of two, was murdered at the Burgersfort Monument at Wagon Hill, near Kliprivier. She was with a male friend when Dube happened to come across them and probably saw an opportunity to get money. Her companion presumably ran away. Dube left her body next to the monument. A few large stones lay next to her battered head. The police photograph shows a neat white court shoe lying on the cement paving near the body, in the rain.

Singh was probably the only adult Dube killed. He preferred children, especially boys, like the fourteen-year-old he sodomised in Weenen before taking the child's bicycle and riding off.

The first eight murder dockets were soon joined by another six that had been positively connected with Dube.

Dube was beyond brutal. But it wasn't his brutality that got to Piet – he had seen more than enough brutality in his career – it was the age of his victims. Innocent children. "One never gets used to that."

Like ten-year-old Lukhanyo Kuwane, for instance, lying naked and with gaping wounds on his face and body at the side of Wemmer Pan Road. A motorist found the boy lying there, calling for his friend, who had managed to run away and escape from Dube. A concerned bystander offered assistance at the scene. It was Dube.

When the ambulance failed to arrive, the motorist took Lukhanyo to hospital himself. He died the following afternoon from multiple injuries. A state pathologist testified that Lukhanyo's injuries had been the worst she had ever seen in her professional career.

Later Dube began to use disguises to lure his victims to their fate. He especially liked to look official. Where he found the uniforms no one knows, but he paraded as a metro policeman and sometimes as an electrician.

On 29 October 2002, thirteen-year-old Zandile Masina left with an "electrician" to fetch an electric cord. Fortunately, this time Dube's prayer favoured his victim. After he had raped her on a mine dump he spent the night with her under a bridge, then released her at dawn.

Nine-year-old Emily Banda, thirteen-year-old Ashley Nkosi and thirteen-year-old Dumisani Nkosi were also "lucky" victims – lured away to mine dumps, raped and, after good prayers, allowed to leave.

We are still sitting at the same spot in Piet's car. Dube's charge sheet is a dead weight on my lap. Piet breaks off a piece of dried sausage and offers it to me while his eyes scan the mine dumps. Is he looking for bodies, I wonder. "Mine dumps are such perfect crime settings, aren't they?" he says and looks at me, expressionless. I shiver.

"Anyone who approaches can be seen from the top. Nobody comes here, except serial killers, ha-ha, and the poor policemen that have to catch them. But I sorted them out, hey, I brought them to a complete standstill." Piet smiles contentedly.

The list of Dube's victims literally fills pages.

Dube asked one of his young victims: "Why are you afraid to die? You're going to die anyway."

And another one was asked: "Do you want me to stab you (with a knife), must I kill you, or are you going to act as my wife?"

In court, the fifteen-year-old admitted with bowed head that he had chosen to act as Dube's wife. After he had identified Dube in the dock the boy remarked in a timid voice to the prosecutor, Advocate Joanie Spies: "I'll never forget what he did to me."

Dube showed Piet where he had slept at night. It was a filthy hole between the concrete pillars of a flyover, filled with empty cooldrink cans, old food wrappers, asthma pumps he had picked up somewhere, milk cartons, bags, a dirty piece of foam for a mattress. His shoe cupboard was an opening between two concrete panels. A forensic team from Pretoria searched for possible DNA samples, but found nothing. "Poor guys, to sift through such a stinking mess. Dube had no wife, nothing. I wonder whether he even knew who he was. Just a good-for-nothing who should never have been born. Who killed innocent children."

The High Court trial, with Judge Seun Moshidi presiding, dragged on for almost four months. There were forty-one charge sheets in total. Piet consulted with each of the more than seventy witnesses. Everyone mentioned how persuasive, even charming, Dube had been, and how he would suddenly change into a maniac. A true Dr Jekyll and Mr Hyde character.

In the courtroom, however, Dube was definitely Mr Hyde. Once he even threw himself down the stairs. He kept asking Piet for painkillers. Sometimes he would wear his charcoal balaclava back to front, covering his entire face. Or he would wear sunglasses over the back-to-front balaclava. "Where he found the glasses, no one knows," Piet laughs.

After being sent for psychiatric observation, he was nevertheless pronounced fit to stand trial.

Interestingly, American researchers have found that less than two per cent of serial killers are deemed to be mentally disturbed. But they do present with various personality disorders, which are long-term patterns of maladaptive behaviour that usually begin in childhood.

Piet snorts disdainfully. "I don't know what was wrong with Dube, but he was off his rocker, that's for sure."

Once Dube even took the court microphone and demanded that

the judge step down from the case because Dube was convinced that the judge was on Piet Byleveld's side. He would rather be tried in Cape Town, he declared, because the judges there would have a better understanding of him. Then he threw the microphone at members of the public who were sitting in the court.

When a graphic artist from the press wanted to sketch him, Dube nearly lost it. "I don't want to be sketched!" he screamed. "What are you doing? I'll come over there and throttle you!"

In the end, court officials had to "use reasonable force" – to use legal jargon – to get him back in the dock.

Then, in one particular session of the court, Dube set himself alight.

While the judge was reprimanding him for his behaviour in the courtroom, Piet smelled something burning. The interpreter shouted: "He's burning!" Smoke poured from Dube's clothes. He had stuffed a newspaper under his blue tracksuit top and set fire to it with a cigarette lighter.

"I tackled him and with the help of a policeman I managed to restrain him. He was strong when he was angry and we had to use considerable force. Fortunately it was only his clothes that had burned. While we were cuffing him he kept shouting: "Kill me, kill me! Choke me like you did, choke me!"

Piet gives a lopsided grin. "It was a proper circus in the courtroom. Sometimes we laughed so much, we didn't know what to do."

The cordial relationship between Piet and Dube had long since disappeared. As always, Piet had to listen to threats and tirades from the dock. Dube alleged that Piet had injected him with a colourless fluid containing the HIV virus.

A police forensic psychologist, Professor Gerard Labuschagne, testified that Dube was not a candidate for rehabilitation. "Studies show that child molesters are the most difficult people to rehabilitate," he assured the court. Even after the most desirable rehabilitation programme the risk that the molester will repeat his deeds increases

Dube in court.

Dube's sleeping place.

with each passing year that the perpetrator has an active sex drive.

No rehabilitation programme exists for serial killers and rapists. And no serial killer has ever been released from a South African jail, Labuschagne informed the court.

Dube's motive for killing was not money or material gain. His crime pattern showed elements indicative of a so-called power-control murderer. He used his intelligence to gain the confidence of young victims.

Piet begs to differ from those people who say that sex is the motive behind serial killings. "Sex is a bonus. These people are driven by power and control – complete control over life and death. That's what it's about. The victim has to plead before he or she dies."

In his voice I hear a ring of excitement. For Piet Byleveld it's all about the chase. For a detective a serial killer is the ultimate trophy.

"What makes someone a serial killer?" I ask.

"I've been pondering that for years. Why did Maake kill, for example, while his brother is a policeman? They came from the same home, after all, grew up in the same circumstances. What went wrong in Cedric's mind?"

Sipho Dube told a journalist from the *Sowetan* that it does not take a psychologist to explain a serial killer. He knows. It is sparked by something small that goes wrong in his life. Part of Dube's motivation was his short fuse, and the fact that he didn't have someone to confide in. "When anger boils up inside and I have no outlet to cool me down, I lash out. But when I kill, I smile – that is a serial killer."

As a result of all his investigations Piet gradually began to detect a pattern: somewhere in the growing-up years something goes drastically awry with the murderer's relationship with one or both parents. There is often an absent father and a domineering, possessive mother. This leads to low self-esteem, sexual maladjustment, and the need to make his presence felt. Later, all these feelings erupt in the cruellest ways imaginable.

Professor Labuschagne explained in court that there is usually no clear motivation for the actions of serial rapists but that there is a theory that most of them feel excluded from society, that they are loners without friends or meaningful relationships, and that they might have been sexually abused at a young age.

Dube's aunt, Sibongile Mkhize, had her own way of explaining Sipho's bloodlust. She blamed his father's family, because his father did not slaughter an animal when his son was born.

Apart from the Dube circus in Court 2F, Piet was "nice and busy" in Court 2B as well, where the Zanner trial was taking place. "In one courtroom I had crazy Sipho Dube and in the other one Frank Zanner. I had to focus on both simultaneously, one hundred per cent, and to have all the evidence ready in different courtrooms. Nerve-wracking, I'm telling you!"

Court proceedings, says Piet, remind him of a game of chess: "You're continuously being challenged. You sweat, or you make the defence sweat. Those bloody advocates. They sit there with their degrees, and then this ordinary old cop thrashes them in the witness box."

He learned early in his career that it's not enough to get inside the criminal's mind; he has to get into the minds of the judge and the legal teams as well.

"I might know who the murderer is; it might be crystal clear to me. But the accused must still be found guilty. The judge must see what I see, so that the case doesn't slip through my fingers."

That is why he leaves no stone unturned during his preparation for a trial. For each trial Piet prepares six files: for the judge, his two assessors, the state, the accused and the defence.

"They're all links in a chain. I do the investigation, I see the entire picture. The advocate sees only the docket in front of him. But after many hours of consultation, I know the witnesses. We begin as total strangers, and then gradually a position of trust evolves. I guide the witnesses so that they relive the entire event in court, as it were. In this way, they don't leave out much."

We return to Sipho Dube. He gave Piet a hard time because the case relied heavily on the murder scenes that had been pointed out by the accused and on observations the accused had made to him and the officers. DNA from semen was found in only one instance. The rest depended on Dube's confessions and identification parades.

"Nerve-wracking, yes. And exhausting. But serial killings remain remarkable investigations. No other detective work compares with the challenge of exposing the killer in court.

"Of them all, Maake's was the most difficult case. But this fellow Dube, especially since he targeted children, was in a class of his own."

At ten on the morning of 23 August 2006, a shackled Sipho Dube shuffled into the dock to hear his sentence.

He was wearing his balaclava and sunglasses, dark trousers and white Nikes. He sat down, covering his head with his hands.

When an orderly confiscated Dube's bottle of water, at first he politely asked why – it was only water? Then he began to rant: "I hope you get run over by a car and your testicles are crushed. Your muti is not going to work."

When the photographers wanted to take photos Dube lashed out at them in Zulu: "You can take photographs until your cameras look like vaginas. Why don't you go and take photos of your mothers?"

Judge Seun Moshidi began his forty-five-minute sentencing with the dry remark: "It has been a long and difficult trial."

When the gavel came down Dube was handed ten life sentences, and an additional 114 years' imprisonment. He was found guilty of the murders of Rashunthee Singh (38), Lukhanyo Kuwane (10), Tina Bernardes (11), Nomnikelo Juma (14), Thabo Dlongolo (14), Anele Mbuku (9) and his cousin Siyabonga Mbuku (12).

Nandi Kuwane outside court. Her son was one of Dube's victims.

ABOVE AND TOP: *The murder scene of Rashunthee Singh at the Burgersfort Monument near Ladysmith.*

He was also found guilty of thirty-one of forty-one other charges, including three of rape, eleven of abduction, six of indecent assault, one of assault with the intent to do grievous bodily harm, one of common assault and robbery and one of theft.

As Dube was going down the courtroom stairs, he cursed wildly. In the courtroom there were tears. The families of the victims, united in tragedy, huddled in a group, exchanging phone numbers.

Sophie Mbuku, whose son Anele had been murdered alongside his cousin Siyabonga, had in the meantime lost a daughter as well. The families' lives were in ruins after the deaths of the three children. She still didn't know where the bodies of the two cousins were, she said outside the court, clearly deeply distressed. It was eating her up.

Piet remembers how the Bernardes family embraced each other, and how they came to thank him.

Nandi Kuwane, mother of ten-year-old Lukhanyo, was elated about the sentence, but said, "I'll never stop crying about my son. He was torn away from me."

Sipho Dube is serving his sentence in the Leeuwkop Prison, east of Johannesburg.

Some time after his sentencing, Dube phoned the offices of the *Sowetan* from prison, announcing that he wanted to apologise to the families for what he had done to their relatives.

He wanted to give them a little peace, Dube said in a soft voice. They could come and see him and he would explain why he had been a serial killer for nine years. Some crimes had been for money, but others merely because of the way a victim had looked at him.

Dube wanted people to know: a man can change his ways. He was no longer the same person he had been. He missed his freedom. Life in prison was too rigid. But he accepted that he would die in prison.

Some of his fellow inmates were afraid of him, he claimed.

He had no idea why …

LEIGH – TWENTY-ONE FOR JUST A DAY

Piet Byleveld picks up the docket with the photos.

Leigh.

She's lying on her back, her right arm twisted back.

It looks as if she has just been laid down in the veld. There, between two small trees and an anthill, where the sun shone down on her on 21 July 2004.

She's naked, lying on her back, eyes open, her long hair loose, clean, spread over the winter grass. Blonde on blonde. The day before she died, she had her hair specially done for her twenty-first birthday party. Her skin looks like Italian marble.

A spider has spun a fine web between her thighs.

Field mice have begun to nibble at her calf.

"It looks as if she's sleeping. Peacefully. As if she has no fear, don't you think?" Piet says, his voice gentle. He runs a finger over her face.

"Poor Leigh. Twenty-one for just a day."

Friday morning, 9 July 2004. A cloudless winter's day with a light breeze.

Leigh Matthews, in her white Toyota Tazz, drove through the big iron gates of her parents' home. They lived in Fourways, one of the northern suburbs of Johannesburg. It's not a wealthy neighbourhood, well-to-do rather, with residents like Rob Matthews, an IT entrepreneur, and his blonde wife, Sharon.

Leigh was in high spirits as she drove to the Bond University in Sandton where she was studying to be a chartered accountant. She looked attractive in her denim jeans, rust-coloured sweater and black leather jacket and she was excited, looking forward to one of the best weekends of her life, *The Star* reports.

The night before, her parents and friends had celebrated her coming of age at a Chinese restaurant in Cyrildene. She had turned red as a beetroot when the entire restaurant sang "Happy Birthday" to her. Afterwards, they had had coffee and chocolate cake at home.

Leigh planned to go shopping later, for a cowboy hat for her friend's twenty-first that evening. In her wardrobe hung the brand-new evening gown she was going to wear to her own big party at the Wits Club the following night. The theme was *Pirates of the Caribbean* and Leigh had planned everything right down to the last detail. In the movie, the heroine, Elizabeth, is kidnapped by pirates who want to kill her in order to escape from the limbo between life and death in which they find themselves. Fortunately, as stories go, the hero saves Elizabeth in time, and all's well that ends well.

If only Leigh had been so lucky.

Bond University is near the Benmore shopping mall in Sandton. There's a boom at the gate, the cars are guarded, the students are guarded. Besides, Leigh was extremely safety-conscious. The tanzanite ring her parents had given her the night before was not on her finger but in her pocket – she was afraid someone might steal it.

She was the one in the family who was always making sure that all the doors were locked.

Leigh lived in a safe, well-protected cocoon. They were an ordinary family and Leigh and her fun-loving elder sister, Karen, were ordinary children, as her father Rob would later tell the media.

Between classes Leigh discovered that she had her mother's credit card with her. At four minutes past nine she sent Sharon an SMS, and they arranged for Sharon to fetch the card at ten. Leigh would be waiting in the parking lot.

At ten 'o clock, Leigh walked across the parking lot to her car, as arranged. A friend, Anne Manthila, saw her walking alone. Someone else saw her talking to an unknown man.

How did Sharon and Leigh miss each other? It must have been by seconds, because Sharon was on time. At twenty past ten, when there was still no sign of Leigh, she sent her an SMS. Directly afterwards, she phoned. Leigh didn't answer. Sharon sat waiting in her car as the minutes passed.

At eleven, Leigh's friends, Giselle Clemson and Neal Radshaw, were also waiting for her at Sandton City. They had arranged to meet to buy someone a present. They kept phoning, but Leigh didn't answer.

In the meantime, Sharon was phoning every few minutes. When she got through at last, a man answered. He had kidnapped Leigh, he said. Sharon laughed, thinking that it was one of Leigh's friends pulling her leg, in keeping with the Pirates party theme. But something in the voice made the laughter die in her throat. Her entire body grew cold, and when he said he wouldn't hesitate to kill Leigh, Sharon became hysterical.

She phoned Rob and Rob phoned Leigh. The man answered and in a measured voice demanded a ransom of R300 000. If they involved the police, her family would never see Leigh alive again. The man sounded calm and professional, adding that this wasn't his first kidnapping.

What do you do when you hear that your child has been kidnapped?

You rush to the bank and draw all the money you can lay your hands on. Rob withdrew R200 000 at the Standard Bank in Sandton, and another R100 000 from a bank at Cresta. In the meantime, he contacted a firm of private detectives, Revert Risk Management, and arranged to meet them at the BP filling station in William Nicol Drive, Sandton. They insisted that Rob involve the police. A few minutes later, Superintendent Deon Scheepers arrived. He strongly advised Rob to tell the kidnapper he could get hold of only R50 000.

In the meantime Leigh phoned Sharon and said she was unhurt but she begged her parents not to involve the police.

In the course of the day, the kidnapper spoke to Rob several times. He agreed to a ransom amount of R50 000, which Rob was to deliver at eight that evening at the R558 off-ramp on the N1 highway, near the Grasmere Toll Plaza. After that, Leigh would be released.

That evening, an overwrought Rob headed for the drop-off point with R50 000 in cash in an unmarked brown envelope on the seat beside him. Hiding in the back of his metallic-blue Chrysler Voyager was Superintendent Siva Patchai. Suddenly Rob grew anxious: what if the policeman's presence in the car put Leigh's life in danger? A kilometre before the off-ramp he pulled off the road and curtly ordered Patchai out of the car.

Alone in the car, Rob accidentally drove past the pre-arranged spot. Furious, the kidnapper phoned from Leigh's cellphone, screaming and cursing because Rob hadn't followed his instructions.

Alarmed, Rob turned round and stopped at the drop-off point under the Eikenhof flyover. It was pitch-dark except for the lights of an Engen filling station some distance away. He flashed his lights three times, the pre-arranged signal for the kidnapper. There was a knock on the rear window and Rob tossed the envelope through the passenger window. Go, the man ordered.

Rob drove back slowly while the minutes ticked past. Fifty

minutes later, at twenty past nine, when he had still not heard from the kidnapper, Rob decided to phone first. Leigh's cellphone was off.

Desperately he phoned six more times: at 21:41, 21:46, 21:51, and again at 22:52 and 22:59. As the minutes became hours, the dreadful realisation grew: the kidnapper was not going to release her. After a final call at 23:35, Rob feared the worst.

What Rob and Sharon didn't know was that this was only the beginning. The real nightmare was still to come.

That night, and every night that followed, Rob and Sharon returned home for only a few hours' sleep. The rest of the time they spent at the Joint Operations Centre, or JOC, at the Johannesburg police station. This centre had been specially established for emergency situations in the city. Within hours of Leigh's abduction, a team of fifteen police officers had set up office there, together with negotiators who specialise in kidnapping and the private detectives of Revert Risk Management. Before long, the team had grown to 150.

In a soundproof room, everyone was waiting in suspense for a call from the kidnapper, ready to analyse it and spring into action.

But the call did not come.

Early on Saturday evening, a desperate Rob and Sharon held a big press conference. Ironically, it was the exact time that they would have been getting ready for Leigh's birthday party. What should have been a fairytale had turned into a horror story.

The kidnapper had a slight accent, Rob told the media. The man had said he was from Libya, and would not hesitate to shoot Leigh.

Sharon pleaded: "Please, let her go. Please! We've been to hell and back, and that's only half the journey."

The conference unleashed a media frenzy. The next day, photos of Leigh with her long blonde hair and sunny smile appeared on the front page of every newspaper.

Forty hours after her disappearance, a visibly distraught Rob asked at another press conference: "What kind of people do this to others?

Do they have no pity? Even bad people must have some feelings."

Besides, he said, he and his wife didn't understand. They weren't high-profile jet-setters. They were ordinary people.

The JOC was inundated with calls and tip-offs. There was even a copycat kidnapping, something that often happens after a high-profile crime. Spiritualist mediums offered their services. Anyone who had noticed a blonde girl anywhere at all seemed to be phoning in, and none of the calls could be disregarded. Chaos reigned. During a third media conference, Rob described how he, Sharon and their daughter, Karen, fluctuated all day between hope and despair.

The investigation became a logistical nightmare. Within hours, the cellphone of Inspector Gabriel Hall, the chief investigating officer, could no longer handle the call volumes. Three extra landlines were made available, and a 24-hour call centre was hastily set up, as well as a website for news and messages.

The Leigh Matthews kidnapping turned into a countrywide obsession. Everyone was discussing it; everyone was thinking: what if it happened to us? As the forensic criminologist Dr Irma Labuschagne put it, in an article in *Beeld*, "It makes everyone realise that in fact no one is safe anywhere. It could just as easily happen to me or my child."

As the days passed, the Matthews family appeared more and more haggard in TV interviews and at press conferences. In a moving interview, a weeping Sharon related how guilty they felt to be lying under blankets during the freezing winter nights, while Leigh might be alone in the cold somewhere.

She and Rob supplied everyone at the JOC with takeaway meals and cake. In time they became like one big family. A family with only one goal: to get Leigh back unscathed.

When it was clear that the clues were leading nowhere, the team decided to call in the special task force of the police. They focused on Walkerville, the location of the cellphone mast that had registered the last calls from Leigh's phone. Walkerville is a rural area with smallholdings near De Deur and the Southgate shopping mall on the old Johannesburg Road.

Task-force members combed the area; the equestrian team was even brought in. Rob and Sharon rented a helicopter to search the area from the air.

But there was no sign of Leigh.

Then, twelve days later, an elderly resident of a squatter camp did what hundreds of highly trained saps members hadn't been able to do. He found Leigh Matthews.

On Wednesday, 21 July, Eliot Makhubela was cutting grass in the Thorntree Conservation Area, adjacent to Walkerville and the r82 highway. He and two friends made a living from selling grass for thatching.

As he stooped to cut a handful of grass between a small acacia tree and a black wattle, Eliot noticed a body. It belonged to a young woman.

Eliot ran to a nearby pub and reported his gruesome find to the owner, who informed a group of policemen who happened to be on the premises. Minutes later the police were at the scene.

But was it Leigh? By four-thirty that afternoon the confirmation came: it was indeed Leigh.

An area of fifty square metres around the body was cordonned off and searched for forensic clues. By six-thirty, the generators were started up to provide power for spotlights. A press conference followed at seven, and at eleven-thirty, with the temperature on the highveld at sub-zero, Leigh Matthews's body was taken to the morgue. It was still in the early stages of decomposition and had remained remarkably preserved. Rob, Sharon and Karen Matthews left the joc, distraught, and went home. Their last hope had been shattered.

In the days that followed, the entire investigation seemed to grind to a halt. The search for Leigh Matthews had initially been the driving force behind every feverish minute. Now the gears could somehow not be shifted to finding the murderer.

Bit by bit, information was leaked to the media. And rumours. The Matthews family found it painful, especially when a Sunday paper declared on its front page that Leigh could have been alive if Rob had paid the full ransom amount. It also became known that Rob had involved the police from the start and not, as initial reports had said, only a day later.

The irate response of the police was that all the speculation was hampering their investigation. They were unhappy about reports that cartridge cases had been found so close together beside Leigh's body that it looked as if they had been deliberately placed there.

As the days passed, the media's interest in Leigh's case waned. New murders, new victims, new headlines took over.

On 20 August, the overworked investigating team were granted their first free weekend since Leigh's abduction. Morale was low. They just hadn't been able to make a breakthrough. No one had been arrested. In fact, there were no suspects. Nothing.

On Tuesday, 24 August, forty-six days after Leigh's disappearance, thirty-five days after her body had been found, without evidence of a single day's progress, Director Charles Johnson, head of the Johannesburg detective branch, called Piet Byleveld.

Would he come and break the Leigh Matthews impasse?

Piet was stuck in court with Sipho Dube's riotous trial. He knew little about Leigh Matthews. But, he promised Johnson, he would soon find out everything there was to know.

A new client was waiting.

Piet and I take the old Alberton-Vereeniging Road to Walkerville. He wants to show me where Leigh Matthews's body was found. As we approach Walkerville, Piet removes his pistol from the holster behind his back. "Just in case," he says. "It's isolated around here."

The leather holster is shiny and soft after being many years worn on Piet's body. The Parabellum with its brown butt has been with him since 1991.

"I trust this weapon. It has never let me down. It's going to be hard to hand it in when I retire," Piet says, and I feel him stiffen next to me. It's only another six months before he's due to retire, in July 2010. "I'm the longest-serving murder and robbery detective in the country, you know?"

Old pistol, old detective: oiled, deadly.

As we drive through Walkerville Manor, the landscape becomes increasingly rural and desolate. We turn into Du Plessis Drive. It's a single-lane road with tall grass on either side and a clump of blueg-ums in the distance. The engine of the Mercedes drones softly.

How would Leigh have felt, trapped in a car with a kidnapper, I wonder aloud.

"She must have begun to suspect something. But you know when I think she realised she was going to die? When he made her take off all her clothes. Then it was all over. Can you imagine the embarrassment, the humiliation she had to endure?"

He slows down, looking for a small acacia tree at the roadside. We stop, get out and walk into the veld. He counts his strides. Twelve. "Here's the anthill, see? I always use it as a marker. This is where Leigh lay."

We stand in the tall grass for a while. Ants are scurrying in and out of the anthill.

Some distance away, on the old Vereeniging Road, cars are rushing past. In the distance I see the tall smokestacks of Sasolburg.

The sky is very blue today, the thought crosses my mind.

When Piet took over the case, he was inundated with paperwork – cellphone records, possible evidence, boxes crammed with documents.

What did Piet do?

Leigh Matthews.

The scene where Leigh's body was found.

He gave the boxes one look and stacked them in the corner of his office, unopened. "No way. It would take weeks to plough through all those papers. And what if they sent me on a wild-goose chase? So I told my colleagues, thanks, but no thanks, that's not how Piet Byleveld works."

And Piet began at the beginning. With the victim.

"I wanted to know exactly who Leigh Matthews was. I wanted to know everything about her. What she had for breakfast, her favourite coffee shop, her boyfriends, her girlfriends, everything."

Piet arranged a meeting with the Matthews family. He had barely entered through the wrought-iron gates when he became aware of the forlorn atmosphere, he remembers. "Rob and Sharon were devastated. Frustrated too, because there had been no progress.

"Rob looked me up and down. He's an educated man. He was emotional, but he hid it well. In the light of their tragic circumstances I decided not to talk to the family as a group again."

The Matthews family were well off, affluent enough for Rob Matthews to be able to lay his hands on R300 000 in the bank, says Piet, but it wouldn't have been apparent to an outsider what their financial position was. "They didn't flaunt their wealth – they weren't the ostentatious type at all."

Piet decided on individual consultations with Rob, Sharon and Karen. "Certain police officers had pointed fingers at Rob, saying he knew more than he was willing to reveal to the police. I wanted to find out how everything fitted together."

Piet asked Rob a few direct questions. Did anyone in his business have a vendetta against him? Did he have problems with anyone at work? Had someone put pressure on him? "After my conversation with him, I was convinced the allegations against Rob were false."

Rob reproached himself bitterly, Piet remembers. "He asked me whether he had been wrong not to pay the full ransom amount. Whether I thought it would have made a difference. And whether he'd been right to involve the police. Should he have allowed the policeman to remain in the car on his way to drop off the ransom money?"

Piet told Rob that, had he been the policeman in the car, there was no way he would have agreed to get out. "The police officer should be the one in control. I blame that policeman for getting out. He might have caught the kidnapper."

Piet hesitates for a moment.

"But I believe Leigh was already dead by the time Rob delivered the money at the toll plaza."

The police could have responded sooner to the information that Leigh's last cellphone signal had come from the Walkerville mast, says Piet. They would have been able to cordon off the area and improve their chances of finding her. But all that is water under the bridge.

Leigh, Piet found out, had been very attached to her family and especially close to her mother. They often went out for coffee. Leigh had always achieved excellent marks and although she was sociable, she was not one for all-night partying. And she always let her parents know where she was.

"She didn't drink, smoke or use drugs. She was a model child. Later, there were so many stories about her on campus but I decided not to listen to gossip. I prefer to gather facts."

Piet's conversation with Sharon was difficult. She was heart-broken about her beloved daughter. "I retraced the route to campus with her to determine how long it would have taken her. She told me that Leigh didn't really have coloured, black or Indian friends. Step by step I got to know the girl."

Then it was her sister, Karen's, turn. Piet sounded her out about the stories on campus that she and Leigh had not got along, that they had reportedly been jealous of each other.

"But it was a lie. On the contrary, Karen spoke about her sister with great affection. They used to sit together in the evenings, chatting and listening to music, doing their nails. Girl stuff."

When Piet searched Leigh's bedroom for possible clues, everything was still the way she had left it that last morning. "She was painfully neat."

Leigh's friend Giselle Clemson told Piet that there had been a boy in Leigh's life. "I looked him up, a smart guy, but it had been no more than a platonic friendship. I don't think Leigh had ever really been in love."

Rob assured Piet that Leigh would never have got into a car with a stranger. It made him suspect that her kidnapper had been a fellow student.

Piet also found it strange that Leigh's car had been left in the university's parking lot. It confirmed his feeling that the murderer had been someone familiar to her, someone who had either forced or tricked her to go along with him. An eyewitness had seen Leigh cross the parking lot alone, which means that whoever it was must have been waiting for her at her car.

Piet shifted his focus to Leigh's classmates.

"Rob was the only one who had spoken to the kidnapper. He told me that, when Leigh's kidnapper had shouted at him that night for accidentally missing the drop-off point, he'd noticed that the man spoke with an Indian accent.

"The kidnapper said something like: 'Can't you fucking understand what's going on, can't you fucking read or understand me?' When he lost his temper, the kidnapper had also let down his defences – and Rob heard his real voice."

Piet examined Bond University's registration list for Indian surnames. And sure enough, among the three hundred-odd students, he noticed the name Donovan Moodley.

Twenty-four-year-old Moodley happened to be significantly older than the other students, and he and Leigh had also been enrolled for the same subjects, which meant that she must have known him.

Moodley had enrolled at the university in January, but in April he had quietly disappeared. He'd attended lectures, but had handed in blank test and exam papers – without answering a single question. Then, a month after Leigh's abduction, he had notified the authorities that he would not be returning.

"When I heard that, I thought: Dig deeper, Piet, you're going to find your man."

From the police computers he extracted Moodley's profile. "Those computers reveal everything: marital status, whether you own real estate, whether you've ever had a criminal charge against you, whether you possess a firearm.

"The National Firearm Register showed that Moodley owned a 9mm Taurus pistol, the same calibre that had killed Leigh."

As was his habit when he was brooding over a case, Piet sat in his usual drinking-and-thinking spot.

He remembers exactly how he had sat there: Amstel in one hand, cigarette in the other.

"And I thought, look, the kidnapper must have planned the whole thing carefully. That much was clear to me. These extortion cases are always carefully planned. He must have been somewhere close to the place where she was kidnapped, booked in somewhere, perhaps; he must have stayed somewhere, after all. I told myself that the next day I was going to the hotel closest to the university to hear whether a Moodley had stayed there."

That night Piet didn't sleep a wink. At the crack of dawn he went to the Formula 1 Hotel in Bramley Park, Sandton, where he studied the hotel register.

And then he found the name. Donovan Moodley.

"Would you believe it, complete with his ID and car registration numbers! He booked in on the 6th of July and paid for two nights. Then he left, but returned to pay for the 8th and the 9th. He came in after midnight on the 9th – the day Leigh was kidnapped."

Piet smiles.

"You know, that night I just had a feeling. No one believes me. Everyone thinks I got information from somewhere. No."

Having obtained permission to get Moodley's banking details, Piet saw that Moodley had used a credit card to pay for his stay in the Formula 1.

"From his bank statements I determined that Moodley had made three large deposits into his credit card and savings accounts within eighteen days after Leigh's abduction: R17 000 on the 15th of July, R15 000 on the 27th of July and another R7 000 on the same day."

Piet also found out that Moodley had been involved in an accident with his Ducati 748 motorbike. The quote for having it repaired was R38 800. On July 28, Moodley told the Ducati dealer he was unable to pay the full amount. His words were: "Sorry, a deal went wrong, I can't afford that." Because Moodley was a regular customer, he and the dealer agreed to a discount of R16 000 on the original quote.

Six days after the ransom had been paid, Moodley bought designer shoes for R850 in Sandton, spent R200 on fast food, another R207 in a chain store, ate in a family restaurant for an amount of R171, bought R300 worth of health products and spent R757 at a car dealership.

Less than a month after the murder, Moodley went to Durban with his girlfriend, Yeshika Singh, and another couple. They stayed at the Holiday Inn Garden Court. He rented a yacht and on the open sea asked Yeshika to marry him.

"The engagement ring of R2 969 was almost certainly paid for from the ransom money as well. Of the R50 000 ransom money, there was only R1 500 I couldn't account for. It might have been cash used to pay for fuel."

Piet hesitates for a moment. "This is something I've never told anyone … I knew there had been unidentified fingerprints on a Lotto ticket in Leigh's car, as well as on some brown duct tape from the scene where Leigh's body was discovered.

The place where Leigh's body had been left.

Leigh's nails had been manicured and were still clean when she was found.

"I found Moodley's prints in the firearm database and compared them with the ones on the Lotto ticket and the tape."

Piet gives a smug little laugh. "Those prints belonged to Moodley. I had him then. But I kept the information to myself. For two weeks no one knew that I had identified Leigh's killer."

Piet wanted a chance to follow up a few other leads and learn more about Moodley. And he was trying to find out whether Moodley had had any accomplices.

On the day of the abduction, Moodley had used his own cell-phone to make a few calls. The police compared his calls with Leigh's and established that Moodley and Leigh had been in Walkerville on the same day.

Moodley's cellphone records also showed that he had been in contact with several of his friends during the time of Leigh's disappearance, including his close friend, Koogan Reddy.

"From the cellphone records I could place Reddy on or near the flyover at the time the ransom money was dropped off. What was he doing there at that exact moment?

"And why did Moodley phone his business partner and his sister's boyfriend at the time of the abduction?"

Moodley had also phoned Yeshika a number of times that day. After he had called her at ten past two in the afternoon, Yeshika left her work for no apparent reason and went to Lenasia South, near Walkerville.

"She later told me she had been unwell. Now I wonder: could it have been her nerves that had made her ill? She and Moodley were continually in contact. Late on the night of the abduction they had a conversation that lasted half an hour. What does that tell you?

"I think it was an organised abduction. Other people were involved. I believe there were five of them."

Of one thing Piet is very sure: Leigh wasn't killed where she was found. He suspects she was shot on a smallholding at Walkerville,

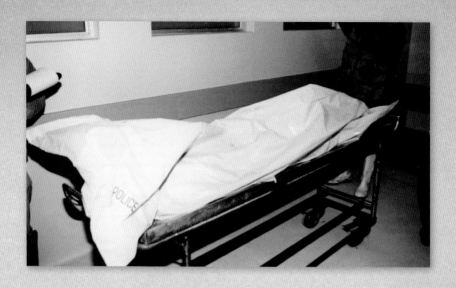

Leigh's remains at the forensic laboratory.

Donovan Moodley.

and that her body was dumped only some time later. It remains a mystery where her body was stored in the interim.

Piet made enquiries at every single mortuary in the vicinity. When he failed to find anything, he cast his net wider and searched everywhere for places where Leigh's body could have been kept in a cooling facility.

"About fifteen kilometres from where Leigh's body was discovered, an Indian friend of Moodley's had a mortuary. I suspect Leigh was transported to the mortuary in a hearse. What could have been easier – they could have driven right through the police cordons with her that night. Who would stop and search a hearse at night?"

Shortly after Piet had begun to make inquiries about the friend's mortuary, the place was closed down. No evidence was found there.

Another missing piece of evidence was the fourth cartridge, the one that had passed through Leigh's body. Piet thinks the bullet must have lodged somewhere, because Leigh was definitely seated when she was shot.

"If we can find that bullet, it will be a breakthrough. Then we'll know where she was shot, and possibly where her body was stored. It's what I'm still hoping for, I'll be honest with you."

Someone tipped Piet off that after the murder Moodley suddenly began attending church in Brackenhurst. In the immediate aftermath of the murder Donovan had even taken some members of the congregation on excursions.

"His father was very involved in the church," Piet says, "but Donovan's sudden attendance was just another smoke screen."

Director Leonie Ras of the forensic division tracked down a former colleague of Moodley's overseas, who confirmed that, after being suspected of fraud, Moodley had left his previous place of employment, a travel agency called Incentag New Directions. Moodley had worked there for more than three years after matriculating.

"They didn't have enough evidence to charge him, but his

services were terminated. The former colleague who gave us the information nevertheless still sold him her 3-series BMW. The payment terms were vague. It shows you the kind of charm Donovan Moodley had. He could sell ice to an Eskimo."

It also emerged that Moodley was a skilled pool player who took part in competitions all over the country. He and a partner had recently started a new venture selling pool tables in Lenasia South and Alberton. Moodley maintained that it was a lucrative business, but Piet found that hard to believe.

We drive away from Walkerville. The highveld slips past our windows. Piet turns off to Alberton; he wants to show me where Donovan Moodley's parents live. Ten minutes later we're in Brackenhurst.

"Here, right here on this corner we caught him." Piet points at the intersection with Klipriviersberg Road. "We followed him from his home on his way to the gymnasium." Piet grins. "Now he's in a different kind of gymnasium, doing different kinds of exercises … "

And right here Piet jumped out of the car, service pistol at the ready, jerked open Moodley's door and ordered: "Get out! Are you Donovan Moodley?"

"Yes … what's wrong?"

Then, looking Piet anxiously in the eye, Moodley spoke the words that would later make headlines in the papers: "What took you so long? I've been expecting you."

Moodley began to tremble, Piet remembers. "He was a nervous wreck. He shook all over as we put him in handcuffs and leg irons."

As we turn into Malherbe Street, he shows me the big tree where they sat waiting for Moodley from five until nine in the morning. Fourth of October 2004, Piet remembers.

We reach the house that belongs to Moodley's parents. With the engine idling, Piet points at the room next to the front door.

Donovan's. It's an ordinary middle-class house with a blue roof. Terracotta walls, a satellite dish, a child's swing, Spanish burglar bars, bright ceramic donkeys on the wall beside the front door.

An elderly woman comes to the open front door, looks at us suspiciously.

"We'd better be off," says Piet, pulling away hurriedly. He puts his foot down as we drive back to Joburg.

After Moodley's arrest, Piet's men took him straight to the holding cells.

Piet grins. "You know what? On our way back to the office I said to Mike, let's slip into a pub for a quick beer. Why? We felt like it!"

It took Piet only three weeks to catch Leigh Matthews's murderer. A hundred and fifty policemen could not do it in double the time.

Why couldn't they?

Piet searches for the right words before he replies. "It helped that I investigated the case the old-fashioned way, using ordinary investigative methods, starting over. I made certain of every detail, by returning to the scene, for example. I think the police tended to depend on information they received from the public, instead of looking for information themselves.

"I did the groundwork."

At the charge office, a shackled Moodley was sitting with Piet's colleagues, waiting for him. Piet left him "to stew for a while".

"When I walked back into the office, Moodley broke down in tears. I didn't want to talk to a man who was crying like a baby, so I left again.

"I had expected him to be arrogant, because some of the girls at his previous place of employment had told me he could be very cocky and opinionated. But there he was, in floods of tears."

When Piet returned after a while, Moodley confessed to everything. Got it off his chest, as they say in the police.

"I'll tell you everything …" Well, almost everything.

232

Moodley told Piet he'd thought he would never be caught, but that when he heard Piet had taken over the case, he became nervous.

During the next hour, the mystery of that day in July began to unfold. Moodley told Piet in detail how he had asked Leigh for a lift at the Bond University that morning. How he had produced his firearm as they were driving out of the parking lot and forced her to drive to a park. How he had tied her up, put her back into the car and returned to the university. How he had put her into his own car in the parking lot and driven away.

Moodley alleged that he had sat in the car with her for a long time near the place where her body was found. When she had wanted to use the toilet he had allowed her to walk into a stand of bluegums while he kept his firearm trained on her.

He had asked about her party, and she had said she hoped it would be a success because she had put so much effort into it.

Piet thinks Moodley then took Leigh to the place where she was murdered. "He was lying to protect his accomplices."

When Piet asked him where he had got the idea of holding someone to ransom, he said it was from a video he had watched. He couldn't remember the name of the movie. It later came to light that it was *Trapped*, with Charlize Theron in the lead. It tells the story of a psychopath's perfect plan to kidnap his girlfriend.

Moodley pointed out the crime scenes to an independent detective, including the place where he had burned Leigh's clothes, cellphone and car keys on an open tract of land two and a half kilometres from his parents' home. All that remained were the zipper of her denims, the underwire of her bra, her burnt-out cellphone and her car keys.

When Moodley read in the paper that Leigh had had a ring in her pocket – the tanzanite ring her parents had given her as a coming-of-age gift – he returned to the scene and found the ring in the ashes. He hid the ring in a CD cover in his room.

A few hours after his arrest, Piet accompanied Moodley to his parents' home. Donovan's father, Stephen Moodley, opened the door, Piet recalls. His mother, Mary, was in the sitting room.

"In his room, Moodley sat down on the bed and pointed out his pistol on a shelf. We conducted the pointing-out according to procedure; everything was comprehensively recorded by means of photographs. In the magazine of the pistol were ten 9mm hollow-point Parabellum rounds.

"Moodley opened a CD box and produced Leigh's tanzanite ring, which he'd concealed in the cover. Before I could ask him about its origin, he confessed that it had belonged to Leigh. Then he took another computer disk from the bedside table and said: '… and this is the disk I told you about …'"

On the disk were letters of apology to his parents and girlfriend, explaining to them that he would be going to jail for a long time.

Moodley asked Piet's permission to talk to his parents. Of course, Piet replied, and they went to the sitting room where his parents were anxiously waiting on the sofa. Moodley squatted in front of them, holding the palms of his hands together as if in prayer. Overcome by emotion, he said: "I committed a murder."

His mother asked: "When? Where?"

Moodley replied: "I killed Leigh Matthews."

His parents were in shock, Piet remembers.

Mary Moodley told her son: "I have prayed every night for the Matthews family."

When she asked: "But why?" Moodley made no reply.

Piet stops for a moment and leans back in the car seat.

"And then it was over. After that, it was a straightforward case. One just needed to put a bit of thought into it."

Piet tried out the car keys, which Moodley had burned with Leigh's other possessions. Her Toyota Tazz was at a showroom, waiting to be sold. Piet was able to unlock the doors, switch on the car, even unlock the gear lock.

With a touch of complacency, Piet says: "That's how you wrap up a murder investigation. With attention to every small detail. You make 110 per cent certain that the case is watertight."

Back home, Piet fetches Leigh's photo docket from the garage.

Elize sits down at the table on the stoep. Yes, she knows that late-night brooding when Piet is investigating a case, she smiles, and that typical "Piet thing" about every tiny detail.

"I've known him to hardly sleep a wink … He gets so tense. He'll walk up and down; I think that's when the planning happens. He'll walk in the garden and find a starting point in his investigation. He says he always looks for the motive first. Once he has the motive, he knows where to start digging."

She laughs. "Let me put it this way, he's active at night. I think it's because he worked such long hours over the years … I always make sure there are Marie biscuits. He likes to nibble in the small hours."

The two of us smile about the image of a supersleuth and serial-killer catcher sinking his teeth into a Marie biscuit in the wee hours of the night.

Living with Piet Byleveld has its perks, she continues. It means you sometimes get coffee in bed at half past three in the morning. "With biscuits, the works. That's when Piet wants company, so I wake up with a smile and we chat. Look, little foibles … he has plenty of those."

Piet returns with the photo files of Body Number 15404. He turns to a photo taken at the morgue, and points me to where the last two shots were fired into her chest at a downward angle.

The room is quiet now.

"She was already dead then. They were fired just for the hell of it."

Rob and Sharon kept asking Piet: did she suffer? Piet shakes his head. "Let me tell you, when the fatal shot was fired, the first one, I don't think Leigh was expecting it.

"I'm convinced she didn't suffer. The girl didn't know what had hit her."

Moodley later claimed he had made her undress and given her a blanket to cover herself because he didn't want to be spattered with blood. A load of rubbish, says Piet.

He'd been standing behind her. ("The coward! He couldn't face her …") The first shot had been fired close to her ear and the other head shot from above. She was still in a sitting position when the next shots were fired.

Moodley used hollow-point cartridges, specially designed to create maximum damage to a body.

The four cartridge cases were arranged neatly between her legs. He must have taken them along and placed them there, Piet says. "When you discharge a firearm, the spent cartridges will most certainly not land neatly in a pile. They'll be spread out over about five to ten metres."

He frowns again. Asks himself again: "Why would a murderer bring the cartridge cases along with the body and arrange them at the scene? So that it would appear as if he had killed her there.

"I think he panicked, because things had got out of hand, you know? The whole country was searching for Leigh. High and low. The days dragged on, and she still wasn't found. The media hype was unbelievable. Moodley had to get rid of the body. That's what happened here."

He leans forward, studies the photos.

She's beautiful, even in death. Between lips that are slightly parted, perfect white teeth are visible. I look at her hand on one photograph, the palm turned upward, the fingers curled, the nails French-manicured for the party she would never attend.

"If she had lain in the veld for twelve days, she would have looked very different from the unblemished body they found," Piet says, poring over the photographs again.

"The body would have been in a state of advanced decomposition. You can't believe what wild creatures will do to a body in a very short time."

He shakes his head, his eyes on the photos. Convinced.

"See how clean her hair is? It proves she was kept in a cool place. Look, there's freezer burn on her toes and one hand. She was wrapped in a blanket or something but the hand protruded and the feet weren't properly covered.

"Those pans in a mortuary are incredibly cold. Any part of the body that comes into direct contact with their surface will be instantly frozen. I'm telling you, that's what happened here. I've attended many autopsies in my life. I know the marks a pan makes on a body.

"Rigor mortis didn't set in in the cool place where she was kept. Only after she was left in the veld. Usually it takes about three, four hours for rigor mortis to set in. But with Leigh, because it was winter, it was about four to six hours later."

A friend of the Matthews family identified her body. Piet refused to let her parents see the photos in the docket.

He points at a shallow gash, visible on the photograph.

"I've never told anyone this. At some point she struggled, Moodley told me, and he pulled a knife on her. It explains the cut."

And no one knows this, he says, but three months before Leigh's murder, Moodley spoke to her on her cellphone.

"It was only one call. Her parents didn't know. I told them. So she certainly knew him quite well."

With Moodley behind bars, Piet began to prepare for the trial.

At the place where her body was found the police had found a piece of the tape Moodley had used to tie up Leigh. Moodley's fingerprints were on the tape. In the back of Moodley's car they found two hairs. Forensic analysis confirmed that the hairs belonged to Leigh.

"The car was clean as a whistle. He cleaned it regularly. But hair is strange. I can walk past you now and some of your hair is likely to be on my clothes. He didn't know that we'd found his fingerprints on the Lotto ticket in Leigh's car either."

The hearing was in Court 2A at the Johannesburg High Court. The trial was concluded in two days, after Moodley had admitted his guilt. Piet regrets the fact that there was never a comprehensive hearing. During cross-examination they might have found out who Moodley's accomplices were, they might have found answers to all the questions and riddles that still surround the murder.

Through his legal representative, Moodley confessed that he had stood over Leigh's naked, bleeding body, averted his face and fired again.

One thing that was refuted in court was Moodley's allegation that Leigh had been shot at the location where she was found, and that her body had lain in the veld for twelve days. A ballistics expert, Inspector Jean Nieuwenhuys, testified that the barrel of Moodley's Taurus 9mm pistol had been only thirty centimetres from Leigh's neck when he had shot her and that she had been sitting on the ground. Therefore, Moodley must have "crouched or stooped" over her to fire the first and fatal shot.

Nieuwenhuys confirmed that Leigh had not been shot where she was found.

Neither did the position of the spent cartridges found beside the body correspond with where they should have been lying, in accordance with ballistic tests, Nieuwenhuys testified.

"I would have expected the cartridge cases to have been further to her right and further away from her," he said. "The deceased was not shot at the scene," he declared with absolute certainty.

Dr Mervyn Mansell, an entomologist experienced in the investigation of crime scenes, testified in court that the police would definitely have found maggots and fly eggs in Leigh's wounds if her body had been exposed to the elements for more than twenty-four hours.

"An uncovered body in the initial stages attracts flies."

To prove his point, he placed pieces of chicken liver at the location where Leigh's body had been found, to ascertain whether there were flies in the veld at Walkerville during July.

"About five minutes after we had placed the bait in the veld, the flies began to appear. During the course of the day we identified six different fly species.

"The fact that no eggs or maggots were found on the body proves that it was a fresh crime scene," Mansell said.

A funnel-web spider and its web, which was found between Leigh's thighs, proved that her body had been placed on an existing spider web a short while earlier, according to Professor Anna Dippenaar, a leading spider expert. The spider had spent only about three hours spinning the new web by the time the body was discovered. The spider would not have remained on Leigh's body for "nine to ten days".

The evidence was, therefore, conclusive. Leigh's body had definitely been moved and had been left in the veld only a matter of hours before it was discovered.

Beeld put it rather cleverly: A spider was a key witness in this trial and trapped Moodley in his own web of lies …

On the TV programme *Carte Blanche*, Doctor Annemarie Mattheüs of the Department of Forensic Pathology said Leigh's French-manicured nails had still been neat, her hair still shiny. "We would have expected to find more signs of decomposition. That's why we suspect she was kept in a cooling facility after her death."

In a moving testimony, Rob Matthews described how "every night before we go to bed, we still step into her room, hoping that by some miraculous act we'll find her there, untouched and smiling, safe and at home. "Our hearts jump and skip a beat each time we go out and catch a sudden glimpse of a blonde-haired girl passing through the crowds – in the hope that it could be her. We catch ourselves wanting to phone her and ask her what we should get Mom for Mother's Day or what she wants for supper."

He said Leigh had been a gentle soul. "When it came to selecting a movie, she would opt for a comedy or a drama, never a thriller or a horror movie. Once, when we were going on holiday as a family, we hired a story tape to play in the car during the trip. After the first two chapters Leigh insisted that we turn the story off." Leigh had not been able to handle the content of the story, *The Silence of the Lambs*.

Stephen Moodley, too, wept about his lost child, and described how the murder had destroyed their lives.

The two fathers were testifying in mitigation and aggravation of Donovan's sentence respectively.

Afterwards they shook hands, *Beeld* reported.

Before Stephen Moodley's testimony, Sharon Matthews said that she pitied Donovan's parents. "Both his mother and father. They also lost a child. Just like us ..."

On 4 August 2005, Judge Joop Labuschagne sentenced Donovan Moodley to an effective forty years in prison for the "cruel and cold-blooded murder" of Leigh Matthews. In addition to the life sentence, Moodley was sentenced to an additional fifteen and ten years' imprisonment, to be served concurrently. By the time he is released from jail at the age of sixty-five, he'll be a pensioner and able to buy his bus fare at half price.

Leigh's relieved parents told the media they were satisfied that it was a fair sentence. Sharon added that she would not forgive her daughter's murderer "in a million years".

At a media conference later, Rob thanked the man who had put Donovan Moodley behind bars: Piet Byleveld. "He gave us a lot of help and encouragement." He also thanked the public for their overwhelming support. "My family and I experienced the rainbow nation during this time." Even minibus drivers displayed posters of Leigh in their taxis after her disappearance, Rob said.

He was genuinely sorry for the Moodleys, he added. "We feel for them. Really. It must have required immense courage for Stephen Moodley to testify on his son's behalf. It's still too early, but there will come a time when we would like to get together."

Rob also said he felt sorry for the families of other victims who had not found peace of mind because their cases remained unsolved. "We are privileged. So many others have had similar or worse experiences, but their tragedies slip by unnoticed."

The public prosecutor, Advocate Zaais van Zyl sc, also said that he found it hard to understand why the Matthews case had made such an impact on the public and the media. "The terrible things that are revealed in this court on a daily basis usually don't even get three lines in the paper."

For Piet the final chapter in the Leigh Matthews case has not yet been written.

"I'm almost one hundred per cent convinced it wasn't the first time Moodley had kidnapped someone for a ransom.

"Look at Leigh's case, for example: initially her parents didn't inform the police. Their daughter's safety was their first priority, so they did as the extortioner asked. I don't blame Rob for not going to the police immediately.

"Moodley's other victims probably survived. Perhaps, because of their parents' social status, they didn't report the incident. The ransom was paid and the children were released. End of story."

Moodley's affluent lifestyle supports Piet's theory. For a twenty-four-year-old student whose only source of income was a few pool tables, he was simply too comfortably off, Piet believes.

He thought nothing of spending R300 on restaurant dinners twice a week, as his bank statements showed. According to the Sunday paper *Rapport*, he spent thousands of rands in shops, pharmacies and restaurants every month. "Shortly after enrolling at the university, an amount of R92 000 was deposited into his bank account. It's a heck of a lot of money for an unemployed student."

Some time after Moodley was sentenced, Piet paid him a visit in prison. "I told him he might as well tell me now who his accomplices were. He became so angry that I thought he was going to assault me.

"I want to know who else was involved. Where they kept the body. I hate being lied to. I can't take it. Don't try to pull the wool over my eyes. I'll get him; eventually I'll find out the truth."

Despite having entered a guilty plea, Moodley appealed against his life sentence. In August 2010, his appeal was unanimously denied by the judges of the Constitutional Court.

The Matthews family established the Leigh Matthews Trust, which lends financial support to the Serious Offences and Violent Crime Unit of the police in Johannesburg. With the money in the fund as well as the R50 000 ransom amount that was returned to Rob, two stress and trauma centres have opened their doors in Randburg and Soweto, providing trauma assistance to community members affected by serious crime and violence who would not otherwise be able to afford professional counselling.

At least something good has come out of the tragedy.

Prosecuting advocate Zaais van Zyl neatly summarised the macabre events when he quoted the Chinese philosopher Lao-Tzu in court: "There is no calamity greater than lavish desires. There is no greater guilt than discontentment. And there is no greater disaster than greed."

Additional source: The series of reports on Leigh Matthews in The Star.

WHITE ELIZE

Piet's cellphone rings to the trombone sounds of "In the Mood": Elize's special ringtone.

"Darling," he greets her enthusiastically. They phone each other six, seven times a day. And every time he says goodbye the supercop adds, "Love you."

"She's here," he says, and I notice the involuntary straightening of the shoulders.

Elize is sitting at a table outside, her blonde hair curling softly over the collar of her black-and-white striped jacket as she looks up archly at Piet.

Piet kisses her and leaves.

It's time to find out where this striking blonde fits into Piet's life.

She smiles. She's known the Bylevelds for years, she says. She and Piet's sister, Elize Louw, have been friends for over a quarter of a century. "We raised our kids together. When Elize went back to work after her maternity leave, I looked after her daughter, Lizé, during the day. I used to drive her and my son, Theodore, to their swimming lessons. I was almost like a second mom to Lizé."

Elize was a regular visitor to the Bylevelds' family farm during the holidays and she became good friends with Piet's brother Johann and his wife, Dykies. Because the two Elizes gave rise to so much confusion, the family began to call Piet's dark-haired sister Black Elize, while her blonde friend became known as White Elize. "So it's rather special, my friendship with the Bylevelds. I've known Piet since my late twenties."

She blushes when I ask her whether she had her eye on Piet even back then. "I thought he was attractive but he was just my friend's brother at the time."

Piet's sister has a soft spot for Pietie, as she calls her brother, says Elize. Through the years, whenever Piet had a chance, he always popped in for a beer. Her home was a safe haven where Piet could relax and watch rugby on a Saturday afternoon.

What was Piet's relationship with his brothers like?

"They didn't exactly stand on ceremony around him, but they respected him and never twisted his arm to stay for potjiekos, for instance. I think they realised he would just pop in and leave. He was always so busy back then."

Piet has been banned from our company for the duration of this chat. He's met up with a few old friends in the smoking room, but every few minutes he's there, fussing around Elize. We send him away with an order for orange juice and, a few minutes later, the waitress brings two Fantas. "The gentleman sends it."

We laugh.

When she got to know the family in the late 1980s, Piet's mother had already passed away, says Elize. She remembers Piet's father, Martiens, as a strict man who didn't say a lot.

Sometimes Esmie and Piet came to the farm at Christmas, but it was always just hallo and goodbye. They never stayed long, she recalls.

"I got to know Esmie, but I can't remember much about her. When Piet left to go back to work, Esmie never stayed behind to join in the company.

"I never experienced her in the group. I could see even then that there was tension, though no one ever mentioned it. The Bylevelds are private people, they don't gossip."

Elize weighs her words, careful not to offend.

Then Piet is back again, making a nuisance of himself until Elize sends him away with a smile and a pat on the shoulder. He's wearing a bright, striped shirt. Elize has radically changed his wardrobe.

At least she knew better than to go "too extreme", she laughs. She takes him along to go shopping so that he can get an idea of the colour scheme she has in mind. "It's still the dark suit and tie, but I've introduced him to stripes and checks, and so on."

Not pink, though. Her Piet doesn't wear pink.

Elize's voice is soft, feminine, but she's no marshmallow. At fifty-one, she's attractive and self-assured. As manager at a short-term insurance company, heading up of a team of thirty, she sometimes discusses the insurance investigations with Piet and he gives her advice.

It's one of the things he likes about her, Piet told me earlier: she's "switched on", inquisitive about life. And she thinks before she speaks, she weighs her words.

When the children began to grow up, Elize says, sipping her Fanta, she lost touch with the Bylevelds for a while, though they still invited each other over on birthdays. During this time she got divorced, after a difficult marriage.

"When the children were young I didn't go out at all, for my son and daughter's sake. I wanted a stable home life for them … I always said I'd reclaim my life the day they left home. Like Piet, I was also trapped in a solitary lifestyle."

In 2006, Lizé invited Elize to her birthday party. Elize was in a relationship, so her boyfriend went along with her. Piet was there with Esmie.

"As usual, the men bunched together, while the women were making the salads. There was music and my feet were itching to dance. Next thing I knew, Piet came across and asked me to dance. Now look, Piet is an excellent dancer, so I didn't think twice.

"While he was dancing with me, he gave me a little twirl, looked me in the eye, and said: 'I'm going to marry you one day.'

"I was quite overwhelmed but I gave him a smile and thought, no, it's just a little harmless flirting."

Piet was very busy with his investigations at the time and Elize had her own life to live.

A year later, Black Elize's son, Werner, celebrated his twenty-first birthday. White Elize and her boyfriend, who had in the meantime become her fiancé, were invited to the party. Piet and Esmie were there as well. But it was clear to Elize that Piet didn't feel like dancing this time. "He was distracted all evening. He and Esmie hardly spoke to each other."

At one point, Elize walked over, sat down beside him and tried to make small talk.

"The chairs were of the kind you normally find in a stadium, with seats that flip up when you get up. When a seat shot up with a bang, Piet jumped. I told him he was like someone just back from the war – shell-shocked. He just looked at me. I could see he wasn't himself."

Later Piet told me that when he heard Elize was engaged, it felt like the end of the world to him. "I could hardly believe I'd let her slip through my fingers. We left the party early because of some drama with Esmie."

A few months later, Elize and her fiancé were invited to Lizé's baby shower. Esmie wasn't there. While the women were having their tea party, the men, including Piet and Elize's fiancé, were having a braai somewhere. They returned later that evening.

"As he walked in, Piet's brother Johann said to me, 'Elize, please tell me you're not going to marry that guy.'"

She gives a carefree laugh. "My fiancé had clearly not received the seal of approval from Piet's family. That evening Piet and I had such a nice chat. He was again the old Piet that I knew."

Towards the end of the evening, Piet put his arm around her waist and looked her fiancé in the eye. "You won't believe it, but he said in a loud voice, 'Don't tell me you're engaged to him …' Gosh, I had to swallow hard not to laugh out loud."

She heard only later that her daughter had phoned Piet that Monday morning to tell 'Uncle Piet' he should take her mom out for coffee some time.

Uncle Piet did.

"And that's where it all began."

Before long, Elize knew she would have to choose between Piet and her fiancé. "I realised: There's something going on here, Elize, and you can't have it both ways; you'll have to make a decision."

Well, in her heart she had chosen already.

"The thing with Piet is … we communicate so well. He allows me to say what's on my mind, without making me feel, oops, I may have said the wrong thing; without worrying that he might have taken offence. I think that's what got me. My first marriage wasn't easy, I was afraid of being hurt again."

Suddenly there are tears in her eyes.

Shortly after the baby shower, Piet had to attend a social function in Pretoria. He invited Elize for a drink afterwards. They met at the News Café in Hatfield, the only place that was still open at that late hour, and they ordered something to eat.

"Those few hours were very special. We drank some red wine. I think that's when it really started … facing each other in the News Café. Something definitely happened between us that night, there was a spark."

Shortly afterwards, Piet told Elize that he had made up his mind: he was going to sue Esmie for divorce.

"I told him to be prepared: divorce isn't easy. I've been through it. He said he would take the chance. I told him I thought he deserved a little happiness."

When she thinks about the way he was back then, she remembers that he was always slightly distant, tense, uneasy in company. He would never mingle, but preferred to stand on his own or talk to one or two people.

"But I think he's beginning to mellow."

At first he couldn't really handle his sudden fame, she says. If people recognised him in a shopping mall and stopped to chat, he would be at a loss as to what to say. "Afterwards he would ask me,

'What should I have said to them?' Then I would always say: 'Ask them about themselves.'"

Piet's first holiday in decades was in January 2010, when they rented a beach apartment in Mossel Bay for a few days. In the beginning he didn't know how to relax, he had no idea how to just "be", she says.

"He sometimes went for a walk on the beach in the mornings. Then I'd think: just leave him to walk on his own, so that he can sort out the thoughts running through his mind."

Elize even persuaded him to go down the high waterslide and to surf. And the reserved detective discovered that it is possible to enjoy a vacation, and just to be an ordinary man.

The first time they entertained, Piet was a nervous wreck, she says. He planned everything with military precision, right down to fetching the meat from the butchery at 14:00 sharp. Elize could see he was highly stressed for fear that something might go wrong, he might burn the meat, or …

"I almost had to take him by the hand and lead him into a normal life. While I was setting the table with candles and such before the guests arrived, he would stand watching me and say: 'I don't know this kind of thing.'"

And later, at the dinner table, she always knew that it would only be a matter of time before he would be setting the cat among the pigeons. And she'd wonder: where does this come from? It has nothing to do with the conversation. Everyone would be surprised, and he would sit back and wait. "I think he enjoys getting a reaction," she tells me.

"You won't believe it," she says, "but Piet doesn't really like conflict. He avoids it. He prefers to leave when people close to him argue. But his family will tell you, when calm has been restored, he'll come back, make everyone sit down and solve the problem calmly and rationally."

Piet with his instant family: l.t.r. Elize's daughter, Virnalize; Virnalize's husband, Christiaan; Elize's grandson, also Christiaan; daughter-in-law Katie; Elize's son, Theodore; Elize and Piet.

ABOVE: *Piet and Elize's engagement on the roof of a London hotel.*

LEFT: *Life is a song.*

Piet seldom discusses his investigations with Elize, but she's often heard him say that he'll never allow someone to get away with murder. Even if it takes years, he'll try his best to expose the murderer.

"He says it with the conviction of a young detective. For Piet, it's truly a calling."

He remains a restless soul, she says. "He'll sit for a while, but then he'll get fidgety and start hopping about like a rubber ball.

"Late on a Saturday evening, when the guests have left, I'll say let's go to bed, I'll clean up tomorrow. But on Sunday morning when I get up, he'll have cleared everything up some time during the night, while I was sleeping peacefully."

Piet joins us. "No more chick talk," he says and stakes his claim. We raise our Fantas. To life. To love.

The two of them are excited. Tomorrow night they're off to London. It's Piet's first overseas trip and a double white treat is waiting for him: a white Christmas with White Elize. They're going to Bristol, where Theodore lives.

But there's a secret that Piet is keeping from Elize.

Somewhere, hidden in his suitcase, is a whopping great diamond ring. It's a finely planned operation, worked out in great detail. Piet is going to swoop. It's time for the blue light of love. On a romantic boat trip on the Thames he's going to ask her for her hand in marriage.

That ring set him back a cool R40 000, Piet told me earlier. "But she's worth every cent." His voice was gruff with emotion.

SHELDEAN – BROKEN BUTTERFLY

Behind the Pretoria fresh-produce market we turn onto a gravel road leading into the veld. We're in a dismal no-man's-land between the suburbs: the sweaty armpit of the city.

There's a menacing silence. In places, the grass is burned black.

Then we arrive – at the police tape, at the manhole, set among bluegums and weeds and rubbish, into which young Sheldean was thrown. If the perpetrator had not pointed out the place, you realise, she might never have been found.

At the mouth of the shaft lies a fresh bunch of pink flowers.

Into this pitch-dark hole, all of ten metres deep, her body was tossed.

Like Alice, she fell into a hole – down, down, tumbling to the bottom.

But there was no Wonderland for this little girl.

The wind gusts through the bluegums, and you know: no one deserves a death like hers.

And no one deserves a life like hers.

"Tuinrand" says the decorative lettering on Sheldean Human's dark-blue school shirt.

It's an ordinary school photograph of a little girl with blonde hair cut straight across her forehead. Big blue eyes, gold earrings, an animated, gap-toothed smile.

She was only seven years old. It was her first term in grade two – a time when the M in her ABC should have stood for Mommy or Mouse – not Molest and Murder.

Pink was her favourite colour. It was the colour of her bike, the colour she was wearing when she walked down the road on Sunday afternoon, 18 February 2007, never to be seen alive again.

Other grade two children in the country would have already been in pyjamas, brushing their teeth, on their way to bed, when Elize Human discovered her daughter was missing. Elize couldn't find her with any one of the thirty-seven other residents at their commune in Pretoria Gardens. Neither was she with Uncle Flippie, on whose mattress on the floor she liked to sit and chat.

She was nowhere to be found.

After a while, Elize went to the police station, while family and friends began to scour the streets of Pretoria. They searched well into the small hours, but found nothing.

The next day more people in the neighbourhood joined in the search. The day after, even more. The whole of Pretoria was up in arms. Sheldean's disappearance touched people's hearts.

Women in pink T-shirts held protest marches. Prayer chains were set in motion, fists were raised against crime in the country. Elize was inundated with pink sympathy. She made the front pages nearly every day, this mother with more mileage on her face than years in her life.

At the commune in Ernest Street, buckets of flowers were lined up against the fence. There were ribbons, rosaries, and candles melting in the sun.

Sheldean Human.

Sheldean's mother, Elize Human.

Elize Human and a friend in τ-shirts worn by the support group.

The police had only one suspect. Andrew Jordaan (26), a skinny, soft-spoken newspaper vendor, had been playing in the park with Sheldean and her friend on the afternoon she disappeared. He was questioned and questioned again. And arrested.

For two weeks he indignantly, arrogantly protested his innocence. He had had nothing to do with the missing child. He knew nothing. He even passed a lie detector test. The police finally realised they would have to release him for lack of evidence.

In a last-ditch effort, Captain Bone Boonstra phoned Piet Byleveld. The suspect was being released the next day, he said. Would Piet be willing to have a go? Of course Piet would.

"One more thing," Boonstra said, "in Jordaan's room we found newspaper clippings about you and the Leigh Matthews case ..."

When Piet Byleveld pointed the nose of his silver Mercedes in the direction of Pretoria on his way to see his new client, masses of cosmos were flowering exuberantly at the Irene off-ramp. He still remembers that chaos of colour.

It was symbolic of his career at the time. In full bloom. After his big breakthrough in the Leigh Matthews case in 2004, he'd become used to seeing the title "supercop" precede his name in the media. He had become famous as South Africa's ace detective.

He didn't know it that afternoon, but in October 2007, he would be promoted from superintendent to director, skipping the rank of senior superintendent – something which, with its strict protocol, was almost unheard of in the police service. Piet was astonished when Commissioner Selebi summoned him to give him the news. His serial-killer successes had earned him this promotion, Selebi said, because "our own" Byleveld was probably the best serial-killer investigator in the world. When the SAPS ranking structure changed, he became brigadier. Later, in 2008, he was also awarded the SAPS's coveted Commendation Medal.

"Just have a look at the back of the medal," he tells me one day. "It says 007. It means I'm only the seventh person in the police to receive this medal." And he gives me a 007 wink.

But here at Casa Piet in Roodepoort there are no Martini cocktails. Only Amstels. His expensive liquor he keeps under lock and key in a special built-in, glass-fronted cabinet Elize had made for him.

Nearly forty years of Piet's life may have disappeared into other people's dockets, but at last the farm boy from the Waterberg was getting his dues.

Earlier, Elize showed me her rock of an engagement ring, set in white gold, and told me that Piet had been so nervous when he proposed that he had dropped the ring. His proposal had not happened on the Thames River, as Piet had planned, but on the roof of a London hotel. Theodore and Virnalize were also present.

Piet had hidden the ring in a red rose. When the big moment arrived, he handed her the flower but he trembled so much that the ring fell out and landed with a thud on the floor.

"And then I said yes. What a perfect moment," Elize gushes, blushing.

It was difficult, however, for Esmie to accept his new relationship, says Piet.

When he retired, Elize organised a party for him on 3 July 2010. It was a swanky affair with 300 guests, also celebrating his sixtieth birthday. A Johannesburg daily published an article about it, accompanied by a large photograph of the two lovebirds.

On his retirement, Piet decided to make their relationship "official". "I didn't want to live a lie any more," Piet explained. "I'd lived one long enough."

For Esmie, alone with Meisie in the townhouse in Weltevreden Park, it was a bitter experience, seeing, on the front page of a newspaper, her estranged husband gazing lovingly into the eyes of another woman. On the day of Piet's party, she poured out her heart in an interview with the *Saturday Star*. She spoke of Piet's "drinking problem" and his "affairs with other women", but added that she still loved her boerseun.

Things had turned belly up when he'd started working at Brixton Murder and Robbery, she said. His personality changed, and he began chasing other women. He had humiliated her.

For all these years, she told *Saturday Star*, she was the one who had stuck with him through all his difficult cases. She, too, had been the target of death threats. "But I went on being a good wife – cooking and cleaning for him, washing and ironing his clothes."

When he read the article, Piet was furious. To add insult to injury, just two weeks after his divorce had been finalised in September 2010, a Sunday paper revealed his "transgressions" with various women, his arrogance, and claimed that his image was not as "Omo clean" as he would have people believe.

"I won't even stoop so low as to respond to that," Piet says and the topic returns to a miserable Andrew Jordaan, sweating in his cell at the Hercules police station, waiting for Piet's famous "confession" interview.

On Piet's arrival, he shook Jordaan's hand – as polite and civilised and humane and calculated as only Piet Byl knew how to be.

When Jordaan realised he was dealing with the top cop of the saps, he instantly became nervous.

"Yes, he got a huge fright!" Piet grins.

He booked Jordaan out. Inspectors Magina and Shezi put him in cuffs and shackles and took him to the Brixton police station.

After the Unit for Serious and Violent Crime in Alexandra had been closed down, Piet had arranged for its members to move into the offices of the former Murder and Robbery Unit at the Brixton police station. Piet himself was back in his old office. He can't think of an office anywhere in the world he would rather work in, Piet says.

At ten past two in the afternoon Jordaan was waiting for Piet in the interrogation room at Brixton.

It was make-or-break time. Piet excused his colleagues, saying that he wanted to speak to Jordaan in private.

"I offered him a cigarette and the two of us sat there, smoking."

Initially Piet spoke to Jordaan as if he were making a new friend. "First I buttered him up and said I would look after him; there wouldn't be any problems."

Jordaan told Piet that, despite growing up poor, he had a good relationship with his father and stepmother. He lived in a back room on their property in Vom Hagen Street. He and his father delivered papers in the mornings. That was how he made a living.

When Piet was satisfied that Jordaan was at ease, he began to question him:

"Andrew, why are there newspaper clippings of Leigh Matthews and me in your room?"

"You're my hero for solving Leigh's case. I've always dreamed of being a detective myself."

"Have you travelled a bit? Have you ever been to Durban?" Piet was throwing out feelers, because he knew about a similar unsolved murder in Durban.

"Yes, I've stayed with people in Durban."

"Durban girls are pretty, aren't they? How do you feel about girls?"

"No, I like girls."

"Do you have a girlfriend?"

"Yes, but we broke up a long time ago."

"And have you had sex?"

Jordaan nodded.

"Have you ever had sex with underage girls?"

"No!" Jordaan was immediately on guard.

"Do you know Elize Human?"

"Yes, I often go there. And I know Sheldean well."

"Now tell me, Andrew, about that day Sheldean went missing … "

Piet noticed Jordaan was sweating. "And he was chain-smoking. I knew then that he was my man, I just had to get him to confess."

Jordaan told Piet he had been at the park that afternoon with Sheldean and her friend. They wanted Kentucky chicken and he – nice guy that he was – went to buy them some. Then they returned to the park, where he played with them on the swings.

A twenty-six-year-old child with ungainly long legs on a swing.

A twenty-six-year-old paedophile on the swings with his quarry.

When Piet asked about Sheldean's clothes, Jordaan described her denim skirt and pink T-shirt.

"What was the colour of her panties?"

"No, I don't know. Oh yes, they were pink."

"Did you push her on the swing?"

"Yes, her friend too. On the merry-go-round as well."

"At the swings, did you push them from the front or from behind?"

"From behind."

"Now, Andrew, how on earth do you know she was wearing pink panties if you were standing behind her? You wouldn't have been able to see her panties."

Jordaan's face blanched. "No, I did push her from the front once."

After they had played in the park, Jordaan took the girls home and left, he told Piet.

"Why did you carry Sheldean home?"

"She was barefoot."

Piet began to put on the pressure.

"But someone saw you and Sheldean at the gate? Sheldean had her arms around your neck."

"Yes, she knocked my cap off my head and I told her she was cheeky for her age."

Piet took a wild chance and said: "Listen, Andrew, someone saw her running after you …"

Jordaan hesitated for a moment. "Yes, it's true. She came to say goodbye and asked to come with me. She didn't want to stay with her mother any more, because she didn't give her food."

"Is that so …" Piet kept silent for a long moment.

Almost paternally, he said to Jordaan: "I can see you're terribly nervous, Andrew. What's bothering you?"

Andrew looked at Piet, shamefaced. "Yes …"

Now Piet confronted him: "Andrew, I know you killed her. I'm not going to tell you where I got the information, but I know the facts. You killed her, didn't you, and you dumped her body somewhere? In a dam or something."

Piet looks at me. "Then Andrew wiped away a tear. And I knew I had him. He said because he had so much respect for me he would tell me everything. He trusted me."

It took Piet three weeks to catch Donovan Moodley. And only thirty-six minutes to break down Andrew Jordaan.

Piet sat listening as Jordaan spun out his story, stuttering, little by little. He had crossed the railway line with Sheldean, Jordaan told Piet, and they'd walked into the veld. When he was certain there was no one near, he grabbed her and pushed his fingers into her vagina. She fought back, kicking him between the legs.

He wasn't expecting that, and he saw red. Furious, he grabbed her by the throat and throttled her. He kept it up until her body went limp. When he saw she was dead, he pushed his fingers into her vagina again.

Later he tossed her down a manhole.

"I kept bombarding him: Did you rape her as well? He kept denying, though I'm convinced he did."

Jordaan agreed to point out the crime scene. He wanted to get it off his chest because it bothered him, he confessed to Piet in tears.

Piet arranged for a police photographer, and Captain Mike van

Aardt agreed to oversee the pointing-out process in his capacity as an independent officer.

At a distance, Piet followed them from Brixton to Pretoria. He was worried because it was getting late and he wanted to find the body while there was still some daylight left.

While he was waiting for Jordaan to point out the scene, Piet parked under a tree. He stood in the shade, smoking one cigarette after another to pass the time.

"I was going out of my mind. At half past five Mike phoned. Relief. Jordaan had done the pointing out. But there was no sign of Sheldean's body at the entrance to the manhole."

Later, on a photograph from the docket, I look at a tearful Jordaan pointing at the manhole.

In the failing light, Piet followed Van Aardt's directions to a place behind the Pretoria Technikon, from where he continued along a gravel road.

Piet waited until Van Aardt had left with Jordaan. "If he caught even a fleeting glimpse of me at the murder scene, he could claim in court that he had been intimidated."

Night began to fall. Piet searched, but found no sign of the body.

Then he became aware of a smell he knew only too well. The unmistakable smell of a decomposing body. Sheldean. She was there, he knew it.

Hurriedly Piet sent for the dog unit which was stationed in Soshanguve. Spotlights were erected. The men were lowered on ropes to the bottom of the manhole.

No sign of her there either.

A large stormwater pipe led away from the hole, they noticed. They followed the pipe to where it ended.

She wasn't there.

But about forty metres further, the dogs became frantic. They had found something.

She was lying on her stomach. Sheldean.

This old sniffer dog's nose literally led him to the little victim.

Piet immediately took control of the crime scene. It was cordonned off with yellow police tape, and police officers kept guard. No one besides Piet and the forensic experts was allowed entry.

"Sheldean's body was swollen; in places the skin was broken. The water and two weeks of hot weather had accelerated the decomposition process. Her face was unrecognisable. The only way we could identify her was by one gold earring and her denim skirt. And a tuft of blonde hair over her left ear."

Piet arranged for Superintendent André Neethling, who knew Elize Human personally, to fetch her from Ernest Street. They took her to the provisional control room at the Hercules police station, where he and a chaplain broke the news to her. Hysterical, she ran blindly down Sannie Street. They finally had to drive her to hospital in a police car and have her admitted.

Her little china doll – as she referred to Sheldean – was broken.

Piet arranged for Elize's friend, a nurse, to identify the body. "I didn't want the aunt or the mother to do it. Rather not."

Under the spotlights, the forensic team inspected every millimetre of the ditch for hair, blood – anything that could possibly be linked to the crime. Piet stood by, continually reminding the men what to watch out for.

At ten they called it a night. Sheldean's body was removed from the stormwater ditch and loaded into the upright white hearse for transport to the Pretoria morgue.

Early the next morning the forensic team was back. Shortly afterwards they found Sheldean's pink shirt and torn panties, in the mud, halfway down the drainage pipe.

A day later, on 7 March, Piet drove to Pretoria in the early morning to attend Sheldean's autopsy. "I was curious to see whether the pathologists, against all expectations, could determine the cause of death. And whether she had been raped."

Body 369/07 lay on the shiny autopsy table. "It was hopeless. When the doctor started with the post-mortem, her head came off. It couldn't even be determined whether the fragile neck bones had been broken. We had to rely on Jordaan's confession: death by strangulation. Neither was it possible to establish whether she had been sexually abused. No DNA evidence was found during the post-mortem or earlier, at the murder scene."

Piet remained in control of the case until Jordaan's first court appearance, after which he handed over the docket to Mike van Aardt to prepare it for the trial.

The trial began on 25 March 2008. Andrew Jordaan sat in the dock in the Pretoria High Court like Rodin's *Thinker*, chin in hand.

In his other hand was a copy of the Quiet Time Bible for Men. He smiled broadly at the reporters filing into the courtroom. His family came over to chat. He was suddenly a celebrity, basking in the spotlight.

Madelein Herbst, who lived in a flat on the same property as Jordaan, testified that he had knocked on her door at half past seven that Sunday evening. He was trembling, quite beside himself. When she asked what had happened, he said that he had beaten up a cop after the police had searched him for drugs and slapped him around.

Outside the court it was a circus at times. There were hundreds of protesters in pink T-shirts and hordes of photographers; posters with slogans like "Burn, bastard, burn!" were waved in the air while Jordaan's photograph was set alight. And at the centre was the grieving mother in a new fiery red hairdo, mourning stiff-lipped behind her dark glasses, clad in a pink T-shirt with Sheldean's school photograph printed on the front.

A benefactor had donated a car, Sheldean's funeral had been paid for in full, and donations were pouring in.

Piet was in court every day during the hearing. "As the days passed, a different picture emerged of young Sheldean."

She was not just the bubbly pink poppet her mother had presented to the world. Barely a week before she died, she had fainted from hunger while at school. She was apparently given only three meals a week at home, and she survived on the school's lunches. Sheldean was a neglected little girl.

Don't ask about everything that happened to Sheldean in her short life, Elize Human told me in an interview shortly after Andrew Jordaan had been charged with her daughter's murder. To the question whether Sheldean had been abused before, her mother replied, "No comment," and added that everything her young daughter had had to endure touched a raw nerve in her.

Besides photos and press cuttings of Piet and Leigh Matthews in Jordaan's back room, there were books and files with photographs of naked women, most of them blonde. On one photo the subject's genital area was covered with a photo of a different person's genitals, without any pubic hair. Andrew appeared to have liked blonde girls – very young blonde girls.

Sheldean's little friend, who had been at the park with her that afternoon, testified in a separate room. Afterwards, she was brought into the courtroom to identify Jordaan. When she saw him she turned sharply but a moment later she pointed a small finger straight at Jordaan.

According to the head social worker of the police, Captain L'Marie Strauss, Jordaan had been indecently assaulting this child since the age of seven. This had carried on for six months, until Sheldean's disappearance.

The friend's evidence was damning, Piet says. She testified that she'd seen Jordaan look at Sheldean's panties in the park. Twice she had told Sheldean "to sit properly". She felt sure that "Andrew was going to take her to his room and to his bed, because I could see that he liked watching her vissie [little fish]," she told the social worker.

This poor child – the victim who survived – never told her mother about the abusive behaviour of Jordaan, who was also her godfather. Neither did she want her mother to see her statement or be present in court while she was testifying.

Just like Sheldean's sad life story, this little girl's story also unfolded in court. She too had been let down by society.

Most appalling was that her mother, in spite of the shocking revelations continued to believe irrevocably in Jordaan's innocence. After Jordaan had been sentenced, she went up to him and kissed him. Afterwards she said that she would always believe in his innocence. Sheldean's young friend was later removed from her parents' care.

Andrew Jordaan's advocate testified that Jordaan had had no proper care as a child. He had attended a special school, his mother had a drinking problem and he was later placed in foster care. He was an outcast, and always more at home in the company of children than adults.

Like his two victims, Jordaan was a product of his circumstances.

"That may be," Piet mutters. "But there is always a choice. No matter how appalling your circumstances have been, how cruelly you were abused as a child, you can still choose whether you want to break the pattern. Or perpetuate it."

Professor Wicus Coetzee, the clinical psychologist who evaluated Jordaan, testified that Jordaan was a paedophile, according to the diagnostic criteria specified in the DSM-IV manual for mental disorders. An IQ test showed that his intellectual ability was extremely low.

Professor Coetzee later told *Beeld* that he suspected that Jordaan's low intelligence, in conjunction with his emotional immaturity, had resulted in an inability to attract the interest of mature women. He had probably experienced rejection from them, and found acceptance in the company of children.

Professor Susan Kreston of the Free State University's Centre for Psychology and Law said in a presentation that seventy-two per cent of condemned paedophiles in prison showed no remorse. They would do it again. She doesn't believe that paedophilia is hereditary, however. "They can choose not to offend. Paedophilia is not genetic. It's not in your blood. It's a choice," she stressed.

Neither does Kreston believe that adult sexual transgressors can be completely rehabilitated. There is no successful treatment. There is no sense in therapy anyway if the offender does not admit his or her guilt, she said.

In an article in *Beeld*, Coetzee was reported to have said that in the course of three interviews Jordaan did not once admit that he knew anything about Sheldean's death. It was like talking to a brick wall. He showed no emotion, though he cried now and then, sometimes inappropriately.

Jordaan admitted that he had smoked dagga on the morning of Sheldean's disappearance. With his low IQ and emotional immaturity, he had not been able to control his impulses when Sheldean kicked him in the crotch.

Acting Judge Chris Eksteen praised Piet for his excellent testimony, as well as his team's professional handling of the case. If it hadn't been for Piet, Andrew Jordaan would have walked out of the Hercules police station a free man. The police had had no DNA evidence to link him with the murder. Prior to his confession to Piet there had been only circumstantial evidence linking him to the child's disappearance.

Judge Eksteen rebuked Sheldean's mother, Elize, for her lack of responsibility as a parent. In his testimony, Jordaan repeated what he had intially told Piet – that Sheldean had wanted to go with him "because she didn't get love and food at home".

Eksteen asked whether that was not where the problem had originated: in her parents' home. When the state prosecutor, Advocate André Fourie, and Jordaan's legal representative, Advocate Philemon Tlouane, pointed out the lack of parental supervision, Elize Human stormed out of the courtroom in tears.

On 9 June 2008, Andrew Jordaan was handed a life sentence for the murder of Sheldean, an additional three years for abduction and ten years for attempted rape. For the rape of his godchild, he was sentenced to fifteen years plus an additional five for indecent assault. He will spend twenty-five years behind bars before he'll be allowed to apply for parole, which will not necessarily be granted.

In a bizarre statement, Andrew Jordaan's elder sister, Jacqueline Nortjé, told *Beeld* that it was impossible for her brother to have done the deeds of which he'd been found guilty. He loved children, she said. "At home, the children were always around him," she said, "and he was always around them."

She couldn't have hit the nail more squarely on the head.

Outside the court, an uncharacteristically thrilled Piet Byleveld told the media he was satisfied with the sentence. "Andrew Jordaan is not the kind of man who should be out on the street," he said in the dry cop-speak so typical of Piet.

Now, three years later, he looks at me and smiles. A sad smile. Perhaps it's just as well he never had children, he says. He would have gone out of his mind with worry every time they set foot out of doors.

Instead, he catches the murderers of other parents' children.

With his retirement imminent, this may have been his last big case. And, ironically, the victims were innocent children.

Pastor Philip Kruger, minister to many in the Pretoria Central Prison, took Andrew Jordaan under his wing. Early in 2010 he told me that Jordaan was always alone during visiting hours. No one came to see him. When he did get a visitor, it was inevitably someone who had "befriended" him through the post. The person would arrive, take one look at Jordaan through the window and leave. Just to be able to boast: I saw Sheldean's killer.

"What a pathetic human being," Piet says, pushing aside Jordaan's files and dockets. Case closed.

Later, in the early evening, as I'm driving back to Pretoria, Piet phones. Where are you now? Have you locked your doors? Phone me as soon as you arrive.

I forget. An hour later he phones again. The initial panic in his voice changes to annoyance.

He knows what can happen on the road, after all, what lies waiting round the bend, what lurks in manholes.

Those eyes have seen it all.

Piet Byleveld with Nelson Mandela.

Epilogue

When Piet Byleveld awoke on 1 July 2010, the first morning after his retirement, reality hit him like a sledgehammer: he was no longer a policeman.

He got up, stood around and wondered what he should do. An empty, murderless day lay ahead of him. A tremor started in his knees.

So Piet Byl walked to his wardrobe and – like every day for the past 39 years – put on a suit. He picked the dark one with the stripes, the one he had worn on the day of his big meeting with Madiba.

For 1 July 2010 was, after all, the first day of the rest of his life, as they say.

Would this man, who cannot sit still for even ten minutes, cope with the diminished demands of his next job title? Pensioner …

It's now a year later. Against all expectations, Piet Byleveld has had a successful retirement. In the evenings he even goes for a walk around the block with Seuntjie.

Together with his former colleague and friend, Major General Bushie Engelbrecht, he now does investigations and consultation work for the private security company CSS Tactical.

He is busier than ever. People contact him from far and wide for advice on unsolved murder cases. As always, his cellphone does not stop ringing. He barks "Byleveldmirrag" into the phone and then turns his head sideways, looking into the distance and listening. As always.

Now that he doesn't have to herd criminals day in and day out, he farms with Bonsmara and Huguenot cattle on his brother's farm. If he has half a chance, he gets the Ranger washed, puts on his hat and then it's pedal to the metal off to the farm with Elize. They listen to soothing music, the window slightly open for the cigarette smoke. And once they are back in town, he has the Ranger washed again.

On 3 December 2011 wedding bells will sound for Piet and

White Elize. Whether the wedding reception will be on a romantic Boland wine farm or somewhere deep in the Waterberg is still an unresolved logistical arrangement.

"Case still open," he says and winks at me.

But it is just a question of time. This, too, will everntually get the Byleveld stamp: case closed.

Acknowledgements

I would like to thank the following persons for their assistance: the Byleveld family, specifically Elize Louw and Elize Smit for their hospitality and help with background information and photos; Book doyenne Hettie Scholtz, who put the manuscript on track so securely; Anne-Marie Mischke for her dedicated editing and enthusiasm; Advocate André de Vries, who made his garden cottage and offices available during the research; Leonie Klootwyk of *Beeld* for her help in tracing archive photos; the SAPS of Kranskop, specifically Timothy Steyn, for obtaining dossier photos and information on Bongani Mfeka; Harold and Birgit Streibel for background on Sibille Zanner; Captain Mike van Aardt and Advocate Gerrit Roberts for background on Piet Byleveld; Elsa Silke for the English translation; my editors Frederik de Jager and Fourie Botha for bearing with their first-time author; Di Simmonds for her fine eye on the English manuscript; Jan and Zak Retief for their patience; and Izak Retief – my compass who always finds true north.

HR
July 2011

And a word from Piet Byleveld

My first heartfelt thanks go to Elize, my fiancée, for her constant support and love. I dedicate my life's work to you.

I would also like to thank all my colleagues, members of the justice system, friends and family for their contribution to my success. There are too many people to mention by name, and of course there is the possibility of leaving someone out.

Being a member of the South African Police Service has been much more than just a profession to me. It has been my passion. Being responsible for justice in a country burdened with the second highest crime levels in the world has kept me awake and alert at all times – and 100% accountable to each and every citizen of South Africa who expects and deserves to be protected and served. It has also given me an attitude of zero tolerance towards criminals, regardless of the crime.

My decision not to study theology but to join the police force instead is one that I have never regretted. I may not be on a pulpit, but whether I'm in my office, at a crime scene or talking to the family of a victim, I am guided by the same principles of compassion and commitment, and of making our communities and our country a safer place to be.

Finally, my thanks to Hanlie Retief for taking the initiative and for her dedication in writing this book.

PB